RE-
CREATING
YOUR
SELF

Please visit the
Hay House Website at:
www.hayhouse.com

RE-CREATING YOUR SELF

CHRISTOPHER STONE

Hay House, Inc.
Carlsbad, CA

Original hardcover edition, first printing, May 1988, by Metamorphous Press, Inc.
Tradepaper reprint edition, first printing, March 1990 by Hay House, Inc.

Published and distributed in the United States by:
Hay House, Inc., P.O. Box 5100, Carlsbad, CA 92018-5100
(800) 654-5126 • (800) 650-5115 (fax)

Library of Congress Cataloging-in-Publication Data

Stone, Christopher.
     Re-creating your self / Christopher Stone.
        p.   cm.
     Originally published: Portland, Or. : Metamorphous Press,
©1988, With new pref.
      ISBN 1-56170-378-8 (pbk.)
      1. Self-perception. 2. Happiness. I. Title.
[BF697.5.S43S76   1997]
158.1—dc21

                                         97-18249
                                           CIP

ISBN 1-56170-378-8

01 00 99 98   5 4 3 2
First Printing Revised Edition, October 1997
2nd Printing, September 1998

Printed in the United States of America

FOR CARMEN,
LADY OF SPAIN, I ADORE YOU.

ACKNOWLEDGMENTS

Thank you, Jack Schober, for your invaluable contributions to the creation of this manuscript, and for your unflagging friendship.

Special thanks are due to my parents, Elsie and Phil Di Leo, Jose "Lingo" Garcia, Dorris Halsey, Mary Sheldon and Ingrid Watson. Throughout the writing of this book I was boosted by their support, nourished by their love and inspired by their example.

I am also grateful for the love and loyalty so generously given to me by my sister, Mary Nilmeier, and my friends, Albert Cirimele, Janet Dammann, Lisa and Tom Derthick, Andrew Ettinger, Bette Gostanian, Stephen Jacobs, Dee and Dick Lewis, Jon Mercedes III, Gary Nilmeier,

Lori Nilmeier, Andrea Schaffer, Frank Schaffer, Mark Tanney, Leigh Taylor-Young, David Alexander Tolken, Gwen Watson, Roger Westcott, Willie, Mac, the DeSisto and Di Leo families.

Because they contributed so much to my personal growth and happiness, I want to acknowledge the memories of my grandparents, my godfather, Ray DeZago, my uncle, Phil DeNisi, and my beloved friends, Glenn Cavallaro, Jorja Curtright, Charles Faber, Jose Garcia Sr., David B. Goodstein, Ken Lewis, James B. Newton and Wilford E. Watson.

I am also extremely grateful to David C. Balding and the staff of Metamorphous Press for *believing* in the value of my work.

And my heartfelt thanks to my students for all they have taught me. I am especially indebted to those who allowed me to print their "Adventures in Inner Space" in this book.

Finally, I must acknowledge that the principles of *Re-Creating Your Self* did not originate with me. They have appeared in philosophical manuscripts dating back thousands of years. They have been taught in different times and places by humankind's greatest teachers. My primary contributions to this material are in the areas of interpretation, organization and presentation.

CONTENTS

PREFACE

The nine years since publication of the first hardcover edition of *Re-Creating Your Self* have been the most painfully challenging of my life—most especially because I was not as free of the false belief in disease as I had hoped. In 1994, at age 46, I survived a near-fatal stroke in a Dallas, Texas, health-food supermarket. That health catastrophe has left me brain damaged and partially paralyzed. My recovery, both physically and mentally, was greatly accelerated by my using the principles and processes described in *Re-Creating Your Self.*

More than anything, I thank God for my ongoing recovery, that has also been assisted enormously by my loving life partner, David M. Stoebner; by Elsie and Phil Di Leo, the most wonderful, loving, and supportive parents a man ever had; by devoted friends, including Alexandra, Mary, and Sidney Sheldon; Clara Abellard; Albert Ash; David and Sharyn Crabtree; Jose Garcia, Jr.; Dr. Michael W. Hall of Dallas; Dorris "Fifi" Halsey; Martha Dee and Dick Lewis; Jack Schober; Bob and Rebecca Van Dusen; Ingrid G. Watson; and the many others who wrote, phoned, and visited during my time of need.

Now, more than ever, I believe in the importance of belief system work, as detailed in this book.

— Christopher Stone, Redondo Beach, CA
June 1997

INTRODUCTION

Being happy, healthy, loved and prosperous is the only way to live. Yet many people settle for much less because they simply can't figure out how life "works," and what makes things happen. Try as they might, they don't know how to get what they want out of life. I used to be one of those people. You may be one now.

My life got off to a shaky start: I was born in a Bronx, New York tenement, the Italian-American son of a J. C. Penney warehouse worker and a hairdresser. My parents are wonderful people and I cherish them, but like many Depression Era children, they were raised in a paralyzing atmosphere of worry, fear, guilt, and personal limitation. And so I was trained to worry, fear, feel guilty and, above all, know my limitations.

I grew up believing that my shortcomings were many. I was troubled, unhappy and confused. I wanted to create a happy, fulfilling life for myself, but I didn't know where to begin. I spent years trying to figure out why some people have the best of everything, while others get the worst. My religion taught that good and bad things are sent to us by God as rewards or punishments for our actions. Science claimed that we are accidental by-products of a world created by chance. If the world was a haphazard creation, then so were personal experiences. Others believed that our lives are determined by past-life karma or present-life genetics. For me, none of these theories rang true. Besides, none of these philosophies seemed to create peace and happiness for those people who lived according to them.

It didn't seem fair. How could I successfully play the game of life if I didn't know the rules? At one time or another, you have probably questioned the rules. *Exactly how does life work? What makes things happen?* I was still asking these questions when I moved to Hollywood to pursue my dream of becoming a journalist. It was then that I met the woman who was to have the single most important influence on my life: Carmen Montez.

Carmen was a spiritual teacher, and the most loving human being I have ever met. Born in Barcelona, Spain, Carmen was a big, impressive-looking woman with long, raven-black hair, an alabaster complexion and beautiful blue eyes that turned lavender when she wore purple, her favorite color. Wise, compassionate and humble, with a delightfully dry wit, Carmen was highly spiritual but equally down to earth. Though an ordained Christian minister, she didn't tout any one philosophy, science or religion as having cornered the market on truth. Some of Carmen's students believed in God, others did not. Personally, Carmen maintained that it wasn't as important to believe in an "afterlife" as it was to make the most of life in the "here and now."

During our first meeting, I asked Carmen those classic questions, "How does life work? What makes things happen?"

"*Beliefs* make things happen," she answered. "Your strongest beliefs determine your happiness and health. In fact, your personal beliefs create *all* the conditions of your life." In later sessions, Carmen explained this philosophy in a manner that I found to be both sensible and satisfying. At last I was getting answers that rang true.

Wanting to know more about how my beliefs created my reality, I read every book I could find dealing with philosophy, self-improvement, psychology, metaphysics, religion and the occult—in other words, everything from A to Zen. I attended lectures and seminars conducted by such diverse teachers as faith healer Kathryn Kuhlman and est's Werner Erhard. I frequented churches and temples: from Doctor Norman Vincent Peale's Marble Collegiate Church in Manhattan to the Santa Monica ashram shepherded by Siddah Yoga's Swami Chidvilasananda.

I discovered that the life-determining principles I had first heard from Carmen were the philosophical core of many of humankind's greatest teachers, both past and present. Whether it was Buddha declaring, "All that we are is the result of what we have believed," or Christ teaching, "As you believe, so will you be," this message prevailed: The power and responsibility to create the life you want is yours, and you create your life based upon your beliefs. Unfortunately, this message was frequently hidden in strange, complex language, or buried in ancient parables. It was not easily accessible to modern man.

During my years of study, I had taken thousands of notes. In 1975, I worked through these notes, simplifying complex language, uncovering the treasured life secrets hidden in ancient analogies. Based upon what I had learned about how beliefs make things happen, I wrote a simple, easy-to-understand blueprint for personal change. I called it "Re-Creating My Self." Using my blueprint, I transformed my self from an unfulfilled person, created largely by the limiting beliefs I had accepted from others, into a much happier, self-created individual. In all the areas of my life, as my beliefs improved, so did my experiences.

As I began re-creating my self, I wondered, "Are people going to notice the changes?" I didn't have to wait long for an answer: Everybody noticed! They wanted to know what I had done. The smart ones wanted to know *how* I had done it.

Shortly thereafter I changed the title on my notebook cover from "Re-Creating My Self" to "*Re-Creating Your Self.*" In private sessions I began sharing my blueprint for personal change with friends and acquaintances. The individual needs of each student constantly challenged me to make the process easier, more effective and enjoyable. Today I continue to help people re-create themselves in both private sessions and small classes. It was a successfully re-created student who first suggested that I write this book.

Re-Creating Your Self explains how you became the person you are right now; it reveals your natural ability to change, then shows you how to make the changes you desire. This book is written with genuine affection and empathy for my fellow human beings, and with respect and admiration for everyone who wants a better life and is willing to assume responsibility for creating it.

I am not writing this book from high atop some pedestal of self-perfection. My life has been filled with problems to solve, and it continues to present constant challenges. I know all too well that the world can seem frightening, confusing and overwhelming. We live in a society that seems determined to separate us from our sense of personal value and power. In such a world, it is not always easy to believe that you matter.

This book is my love letter to you. My message: You are important and irreplaceable. You deserve the best life has to offer and you have the power to create it.

Re-Creating Your Self is for the everyday people of this world. (But even we so-called ordinary people possess extraordinary potential.) This book is written in a simple style, using simple words. I believe that truth is simplicity itself, and that's the way it should be presented.

Because I don't expect, or want, anyone to accept the principles of *Re-Creating Your Self* on faith, each of the first fourteen chapters is followed by an "Adventure in Inner Space." These adventures give you the opportunity to prove for your self the validity of this book's philosophy. They will also help you to better understand your self, and that's why I call them "adventures"—I believe the journey into one's self is life's most exciting, challenging and rewarding adventure.

However, the adventures are optional. You may explore them, or you may skip them and just read the book. Either way, you will benefit. Many of my students read the entire book first, then go back and explore the adventures.

Now, let's get started. It's as easy as turning the page.

PART ONE

YOU CAN HAVE A NEW LIFE–AND YOU CAN START CREATING IT *NOW*

1

YOUR *NOW* SELF

Before *Re-Creating Your Self,* it's important to determine who you are right now. I call the person you are at this time "your *now* self." The sole purpose of this chapter is to become better acquainted with that person. One effective way of doing this is to write about who you believe your self to be.

Get a 100-sheet, 8½ by 11-inch college-ruled note-book—hereafter referred to as your adventure logbook—and a pen or pencil. On the cover, write your name; then, below your name, "Adventures in Inner Space."

Now, at the top of the first page, write:

ADVENTURE 1

MY NOW SELF

STEP 1: Describe your self fully. Include an emotional, intellectual and physical description. Write about your good qualities and your bad habits. Mention your special abilities as well as your personal limitations. What makes you happy? What makes you angry and sad? Is there a motto you live by? Write anything about your self that comes to mind. But you are not to use other people's opinions about you. The only important opinions are your *own*.

   Don't worry about the quality, quantity or style of your writing. They don't matter. As long as you write your true feelings about who you are, your adventure will be a success. No particular time limit is recommended; do it at your own pace.

STEP 2: After you have written your self-profile, go back and read it. Have you left out anything? Do you now disagree with something you have written? The purpose of this adventure is to define your *now* self as completely and accurately as possible, so feel free to add or edit material as you see fit.

   Even great adventurers use guides. To guide you through this first adventure, I offer two examples written by former students. (Their names have been changed to protect their privacy.) You can follow their leads, but don't worry about tracing their every step. Create a style and structure that feels comfortable to you.

YOUR GUIDES FOR ADVENTURE 1

TIM, 24 YEARS OLD:

My parents had to get married because my mother was pregnant, and I believe that I'm the product of the union of bad things: depravity, anger, hatred, fear and deception. Those evil characteristics are festering inside me, waiting for a provocation to expand to full capacity. I fear that if I don't keep careful control over myself, the real me is going to bound out of my forged image like a devil from under a nun's habit.

Descriptives that come to mind when I think of myself are clumsy, incompetent, selfish and sadistic. I wish I had a nickel for every time someone described me as "strange." (I heard this more often as a youth because I learned to act "normal" as I matured.)

Though I look like an "All-American Boy"—I'm tall and muscular with blond hair and blue eyes—I feel ugly and incapable of being anyone's friend or lover.

I desperately fear I will never be successful at anything...I feel I do not qualify as an adult.

In direct contradiction, I possess an enormous capacity for altruistic love. I have a great need to lift up the impoverished and the ill. I have a deep awareness and appreciation for all things living and inanimate. I have an above-averge intellect, with powers of insight and perception.

I'm anxious to re-create myself because I believe that once I break free of my "prison," the wonders and resources within me will abound.

Meanwhile, I feel like someone who is always doing "it"

wrong, whatever "it" is, always deserving a whippin', and usually getting one.

KATHY, 45 YEARS OLD:

I am a child of God, a woman, daughter, sister, wife and mother.

I have more than my share of faults. I'm not nearly as good, strong, brave, wise, confident and loving as I'd like to be, but I know it's possible for me to be all those things. That's why I want to re-create myself.

I'm more caring, forgiving and patient than I used to be. I'm proud of that. I'm grateful for all the blessings God has bestowed on me, and I remember to give thanks often. I know God wants me, and everyone, to enjoy life to the fullest. I'm not always happy, but out of my unhappiness comes wisdom and growth, so I'm thankful for unhappiness at times.

Physically, I have a pretty face, but I've always had a tendency toward overweight. That's because I can't control my appetite and occasional gluttony. Eating has become too important to me. I sometimes feel that I live to eat instead of eating to live, and that's something I want to change.

My most important goal is to become a better person. When I leave this world, I want it to be a better place because I lived here. While I'm here, I hope to touch others' lives and enhance them. My greatest needs are to be loved and enjoyed. "Understanding" from others would be nice, too, but I can live without it because I always know God understands.

You've most likely seen diet ads that picture the dieter "before" and "after." Think of the person you've just written about, your *now* self, as your personal "before" portrait. After you've completed *Re-Creating Your Self*, you will see dramatic changes. You may barely recognize the person you have just described.

2

HOW YOUR
NOW SELF WAS
CREATED

How did you become the self you described in Adventure 1? Did you create that person? Is your *now* self the real you? The answers to these questions may surprise you.

Note that this chapter is *not* titled, "How *You* Created Your *Now* Self." That's because the person you described in Adventure 1 was largely shaped by the influential people from your childhood. In other words, the person you are right now was primarily created by others, not by your self.

Who created your *now* self? Here's a partial list: Parents. Grandparents. Guardians. Brothers and sisters. Teachers. Clergypersons. Friends. Neighbors. Government. Society. The media. The arts. Advertisers.

When did these contributors start creating your *now* self? They began before you were born. It started with your parents' first thoughts about what they wanted for their children—thoughts they probably had when *they* were children. And, in a real way, the beliefs and expectations of your ancestors, older siblings, teachers, religious, political and societal leaders were also working to shape your *now* self even before you took your first breath.

How did they do it? They convinced you to accept *their* beliefs about your self, others, and the world. They defined reality for you. They accomplished this in both subtle and not-so-subtle ways. By example. By repeated suggestion. By teaching and preaching. With rewards and punishments. By censoring information and experiences. By using fear and guilt to mold you into the person they wanted you to be. And even the most rebellious among you were not immune.

Why did they force their beliefs on you? It wasn't because they were bad people. Chances are they were convinced that their personal beliefs about how life "works" were facts of life. They considered it their responsibility to pass these "facts" on to you. If they were guilty of anything, it was ignorance: an ignorance passed on from one generation to another. Simply stated, most people still haven't learned the difference between their personal beliefs about life and the incontestable facts of life.

You may have been born into a family whose personal beliefs about reality were more negative than positive. Consequently, many of the beliefs you accepted did not contribute to your health, happiness and well-being. Some of the people you turned to for direction were incapable of successfully guiding their own lives, much less yours.

Making matters worse, you were born into a society that believes in the value of "sameness." This widely accepted belief is both unhealthy and unnatural. It is an unhealthy belief because standardization stunts personal growth and creativity; trying to fit "the norm" can cause frustration, depression and self-alienation. It is a downright unnatural belief because nature doesn't permit standardization: No two trees are alike, even among the same variety; no two blades of grass are the same. Even "identical" twins are not identical.

But the human race is going through a phase—an unmercifully long phase—during which most people fear personal originality (when it is "sameness" that should scare them). That's why many of the people who helped to shape your life discouraged individuality and encouraged conformity.

You probably attended schools that did their best to make you the same as everyone else. Teachers sometimes punished you for acting as an individual; they praised you for thinking and behaving like your classmates. As a teenager, you may have compromised your individuality in order to be accepted as "one of the gang." You thought, talked and behaved like your friends. You dressed like them, cut your hair like theirs. You learned to like the same songs, dances, movies and television shows.

Later, when you fell in love, you made your self over in an attempt to be loved and desired by the object of your affection. You stopped (or started) smoking, changed your religion, even learned to like anchovies—whatever it took! In adulthood, you quickly learned that the surest way to be accepted in business, or in the neighborhood, is to become a Xerox copy of those by whom you want to be liked.

Thus you became an *other*-created person: someone who lives according to the ideas and beliefs, the standards and values, of others. You accepted the false belief that if you do what you're told to do, if you don't rock the boat, happiness will be your reward. But it doesn't always work out that way, does it?

So what went wrong with the plan? Why didn't you become the person you wanted to be, living the life you desired? Simply this: Living according to the beliefs of others—becoming the person *other* people want you to be—doesn't create personal happiness.

During childhood, accepting beliefs from others was often necessary for survival. For example, as a toddler it was good for you to accept your parents' belief that it was dangerous to cross the street alone. Adopting the beliefs of others also provided you with a basic orientation to life, your family and society. It served as a direction for personal growth.

The problem is that it is all too common to accept, and live by, the beliefs of others long after that habit has ceased to be beneficial. As you matured, and your ability to reason developed, you needed to start defining reality for your self. Equally important, you needed to examine the beliefs that you had already accepted from others, identifying those that created positive feelings and experiences, and those that did not. Any beliefs that did not contribute to your health, happiness and well-being should have been discarded. In other words, as you matured, you should have changed from an *other*-created person into a self-created person. You may not have made this transformation. *Re-Creating Your Self* will help you do so.

ADVENTURE 2

MY PERSONAL BELIEFS, PART ONE

Adventure 2 is designed to serve two purposes: It will give you the chance to discover some of the personal beliefs that are creating your life (you will explore other areas of beliefs in upcoming chapters); and it will provide an opportunity to prove for your self the validity of this chapter's theory— that your *now* self was created largely by beliefs you accepted from others.

STEP 1: Search your mind, then list *all* your beliefs in each of these four general categories:

> God
> Country
> Love
> Marriage

Before beginning Step 1, students frequently ask, "Exactly what *is* a belief?" In *Re-Creating Your Self*, a belief is defined as *any* idea you accept as being true. So any idea you accept as being factual about God, country, love and marriage should be included in your lists. For example, if you don't believe there is a God, then that *is* one of your beliefs about God. Leave spaces after each belief and after each category of beliefs. You will need this space for a later adventure.

STEP 2: Carefully read the lists you've just made. Remember, you want to include *every* idea you accept as being true about God, country, love and marriage. Have you left out any beliefs? If so, add them now.

STEP 3: Go back and consider each belief, one at a time. Ask your self, "From whom did I first learn this 'truth'? Did this idea originate with me, or did I first accept it from someone else? Did it first come to me from my family, friends, teachers? Did I originally accept this belief from a religious, scientific or political system? Did I hear it in a song, a movie, or television show?" Following each belief on your lists, write the original source of your belief.

YOUR GUIDE FOR ADVENTURE 2

MARK, 35 YEARS OLD:

The following represents Mark's adventure *after* completing the three steps suggested above.

GOD
1. **Belief**: *God is all-powerful and perfect.* **Source of belief**: *my minister.*
2. **Belief**: *Jesus was God. He died for my sins.* **Source of belief**: *my minister.*
3. **Belief**: *I'm an unworthy sinner.* **Source of belief**: *my minister.*
4. **Belief**: *I'll only get what I want if God wants me to have it.* **Source of belief**: *my mother.*

COUNTRY

1. **Belief:** The United States is the greatest country in the world. **Source of belief:** my father.
2. **Belief:** If asked, I should be willing to give my life for my country. **Source of belief:** my third-grade teacher.
3. **Belief:** The Russians want to bury us. **Source of belief:** Nikita Krushchev.
4. **Belief:** Most politicians are more concerned about their careers than their constituents. **Source of belief:** myself.

LOVE

1. **Belief:** I must prove myself worthy of love. I must earn it. **Source of belief:** my mother.
2. **Belief:** Some people just aren't lovable. **Source of belief:** myself.
3. **Belief:** Sometimes love doesn't last forever. **Source of belief:** my parents. (They explained this to me after their divorce.)
4. **Belief:** The better you look, the better chance you have of being loved. **Source of belief:** ads, TV and radio commercials, movies and television shows.

MARRIAGE

1. **Belief:** Half of all marriages fail. **Source of belief:** I read it somewhere.
2. **Belief:** Marriage is a 50/50 proposition. **Source of belief:** my father. (After the divorce, he said my mother hadn't done her 50 percent.)
3. **Belief:** Married people end up deceiving each other. **Source of belief:** my older brother and his wife. (Later, I learned it for myself in my own marriage.)
4. **Belief:** You give up your freedom when you marry. **Source of belief:** my father.
5. **Belief:** Sooner or later, married people get bored with each other. **Source of belief:** myself.

Mark had accepted fourteen of the eighteen beliefs on his list from others; admittedly, he had done so without carefully examining or evaluating these ideas for himself. That made Mark's *now* self more than 75 percent *other-*created in the four belief categories explored. Little wonder he was chronically depressed and self-alienated: His frequent lament was, "I just don't know who I am anymore!"

Most of my students discover that their *now* selves are at least 50 percent *other-*created. How many of the beliefs you have listed were first accepted from others?

3

YOU ARE WHO YOU *BELIEVE* YOU ARE

The following ideas are among the most important in this book. They are the heart and soul of *Re-Creating Your Self*:

- Your beliefs create your life.
- You are who you *believe* you are.
- The world is what you believe it to be.

- In *all* areas of your life, your beliefs create your personal experiences.
- You can re-create your self and change your life by changing your beliefs.

Before continuing, read those statements again. Read them slowly. Let the words sink in. Think about their meaning. Consider the implications.

Your beliefs create your life and all of its conditions. I mean for you to take this *literally*.

Your life is *not* controlled by the gods, the fates or the stars. You are *not* the puppet of a manipulative Creator, or the by-product of an accidentally created world. Your life is *not* determined by heredity, nor are you the victim of past lives, an indentured spiritual slave paying off a karmic debt. You are *not* at the mercy of your fellow man, or even your own unconscious desires.

You *are* at the mercy of your own beliefs about your self, others, and the world. That means you can be as happy, healthy and prosperous as you *believe* you can be. You are limited only by the limitations of your personal beliefs.

Success is not a secret, it is a system—a positive belief system. If you're unhappy with your self, you can change your beliefs, and in so doing, change your world. Pre-destination is a myth. Life is an experiment in the use of free will and personal creativity. As I advise my students who believe in a Supreme Being, "Thank God for giving you life, but thank *your self* for the life you have."

Whatever your beliefs, sooner or later they will materialize as personal experiences. That doesn't mean you will eventually get everything you want. Your *beliefs* and your *desires* are often two different things. You create your experiences in line with your *beliefs*, not your desires. If you desire a peaceful life but you believe, "Life's a struggle!" you will create the strife that you believe in, not the peace you desire.

If life is what you make it, then your beliefs are what "make" or create your life. Placebos work if you believe in them. Voodoo is effective if you believe in black magic; it fails to affect you if you don't. You may be cured at Lourdes if you truly believe you will be healed.

The media regularly report stories similar to one that recently came out of a London hospital. A study of over 100 patients revealed that *any* treatment will significantly reduce back pain—as long as the patient *believes* he's receiving a treatment that will help. In this study, even a majority of the patients who received no actual treatment, but *believed* they had received beneficial treatment, told doctors they were feeling much better.

Once I understood that beliefs make things happen, it was easy for me to trace how my beliefs had formed my personal experiences, and how the beliefs of my family and friends had determined theirs. For example, the philosophy of one friend is, "Life is a series of ups and downs." And that's exactly how he creates his life—spurts of success are followed by periods of dire hardship. As long as he believes that he must plunge to the bottom after soaring to the top, his life will be a dizzy roller-coaster ride. In other words, his belief that "life is a series of ups and downs" actually creates the "downs." On the other hand, I have a friend who doesn't believe in setbacks. He believes that he builds upon each success, and so his life is a continuing pyramid of progress and prosperity.

Our personal experiences almost always *seem* to confirm what we believe to be "true" and "factual," but it's our beliefs that create those experiences. It's not the other way around.

You can trace for your self how the prevailing beliefs of your family and friends form their private reality: How about the relative who fervently *believes* in her own poor health and thus creates chronic illnesses? Then there's the buddy who effortlessly climbed the ladder of success because he didn't *believe* he could fail. And what about the lonely friend who wants to marry but remains single, because she *believes* herself to be unattractive and unworthy of love?

THERE ARE NO ACCIDENTS

Students commonly ask, "If personal beliefs cause my experiences does that mean I create illnesses and accidents, too?"

My answer is an emphatic, "Yes!"

Illnesses are outer manifestations of inner needs, "dis-ease," or beliefs. I'm not saying that you consciously decide, "Tomorrow morning I'm going to awaken with a cold that will prevent me from going to work (or school)." I'm saying that no illness comes to you arbitrarily; some purpose is served.

As for so-called accidents, they aren't accidents at all; they, too, are created in line with personal beliefs. For example, imagine that you and your neighbor both work nights. You both walk home alone in the wee hours. You are mugged twice in one year; your neighbor remains unharmed. You may ask your self, "Why was *I* mugged? What did *I* do to deserve this?"

Look to your beliefs for the answer. Upon examining them, you may find that you believe people are basically evil. The muggings, then, were no accident. They were the physical manifestation of your belief in man's evil nature. Your negative belief attracted those experiences as if you were a magnet for muggers.

Your neighbor, on the other hand, believes that people are basically good. She got home safely every night, and that's not just dumb luck. Her positive experience was the materialization of her belief in man's inherent goodness. Her positive belief acted as a protective shield.

Using the same example, perhaps you don't believe man is evil, but maybe you're feeling guilty about doing something dishonest at work. You may then have created the mugging in line with the belief that you deserve to be punished for your dishonesty. Your need to be punished attracted a mugger with a need to punish.

Life is a cooperative venture. We are in league with one another, and not in conflict. A self-described "victim" will effortlessly attract a victimizer; a person who is ready to receive love will always find someone who is ready to give love. An old proverb puts it this way, "When the student is ready, the teacher appears." The laws of attraction and cooperation are inevitable and automatic.

Students always want to know, "How can a belief create a physical experience?" Briefly, here's how it works: A belief possesses energy. Dictionaries define energy as "life"..."power in action"..."the ability to create an effect." Your belief, then, possesses "life," a "power in action" that has "the ability to create an effect." The effect your belief creates is called a physical experience. In other words, a physical experience is a belief, materialized.

You are a student enrolled in a "schoolhouse" called Earth. The curriculum includes creativity, self-understanding and personal development. In Schoolhouse Earth, the way you learn about your self is by creating physical experiences based upon your personal beliefs. Your experiences, then, are like report cards; they indicate how well you are progressing in your personal development.

It's time to open your logbook again. Title this adventure:

ADVENTURE 3

MY PERSONAL BELIEFS, PART TWO

STEP 1: Using the guidelines in Adventure 2 for discovering your beliefs, identify *all* of your personal beliefs in the categories listed below. As in Adventure 2, leave spaces after each belief and each category of beliefs. Some of my students divide this adventure into daily sessions, listing their beliefs in one category per day.

Happiness   Success
Health   Guilt
Aging   Prejudice
Sex   Self-worth
Money   Career
My place in the world

STEP 2: List any other important personal beliefs that don't fit into the categories mentioned in Adventures 2 and 3.

STEP 3: After you have completed your lists, read them over, including your lists from Adventure 2. These beliefs, along with others you have yet to identify, are creating your personal experiences and all of the conditions of your life.

YOUR GUIDE FOR ADVENTURE 3

GEORGIA, 30 YEARS OLD:

HAPPINESS
1. *Belief:* Happiness must be striven for.
2. *Belief:* Striving for happiness doesn't always result in achieving happiness.
3. *Belief:* If you have someone to love and some exciting work to do, you have a good chance of achieving happiness.
4. *Belief:* Though it isn't impossible to be happy alone, it's easier to be happy if you have someone.

HEALTH
1. *Belief:* Physical and emotional health are inextricably related.
2. *Belief:* I am a healthy person.
3. *Belief:* I can afford to be cavalier with my body.
4. *Belief:* On the other hand, the people I love are more delicate (and more important), and their health must be protected at all times.
5. *Belief:* If you do get sick, you musn't give in to it; ignore it, or it will beat you down.
6. *Belief:* Nothing works to cure a headache—except a lobotomy.

AGING
1. *Belief:* If I ever lose my health or my eyesight, there's no point in going on.
2. *Belief:* However, there are advantages to growing old. I won't have to prove myself so much.
3. *Belief:* Old age doesn't necessarily cause decay and senility.
4. *Belief:* Some of the most joyful and fervent people I know are in their eighties.

5. **Belief**: *The quality of your later years depends on what you put into your early ones.*
6. **Belief**: *Keeping your horizons open keeps you young.*
7. **Belief**: *The moment you stop taking chances, lose interest in life, or move in with your daughter-in-law, you're done for.*

SEX
1. **Belief**: *Sex isn't all it's cracked up to be.*
2. **Belief**: *Romance is a million times more exciting than sex.*
3. **Belief**: *The purpose of sex is to get close to someone you love. But it doesn't serve that purpose very well.*
4. **Belief**: *Sex without love is pointless and ridiculous.*
5. **Belief**: *I suspect that I've just been unlucky, and that all my beliefs about sex would change instantly if the right Gypsy Prince came my way!*

MONEY
1. **Belief**: *Having money is a wonderful thing, if you've earned it.*
2. **Belief**: *Because I've never had to earn money, I don't have the right to keep it.*
3. **Belief**: *It's better to give away money than to spend it on yourself.*
4. **Belief**: *Things that you buy for yourself aren't worth anything.*
5. **Belief**: *The only possessions that matter are those that the people you love have given you.*
6. **Belief**: *Everyone deserves to have enough money to live comfortably and with dignity.*

CAREER
1. **Belief**: *A fulfilling career, along with love, is what life is all about.*
2. **Belief**: *If you love your work, you will succeed at your career.*
3. **Belief**: *Talent will out.*
4. **Belief**: *I was born to be a writer and would be a disaster doing anything else.*

5. **Belief**: A traditional career, with office politics and long-term planning, is spirit-killing. I would rather sweep the streets.

SUCCESS
1. **Belief**: Success is being happy with yourself.
2. **Belief**: You must never buy into anyone else's idea of success.
3. **Belief**: To live successfully, you must become your own hero.
4. **Belief**: Worldly success can be a trap.
5. **Belief**: Compromising yourself in any way in order to be a success is a dead end.
6. **Belief**: Doing your work well, keeping content, and making the people you love happy—that's success!

GUILT
1. **Belief**: It's wrong to make someone else feel guilty.
2. **Belief**: It's fine to feel guilty yourself.
3. **Belief**: Guilt is a cattle-prod, pressuring us into more perfect behavior.
4. **Belief**: People who never feel guilty about anything are "Martians."
5. **Belief**: Neurotics who feel guilty about every little thing are generally very nice people.

PREJUDICE
1. **Belief**: I have none of the "traditional," major prejudices.
2. **Belief**: Prejudices are a total waste of time and energy.
3. **Belief**: Prejudice indicates ignorance and smugness.
4. **Belief**: The goal to strive for is to have a mind that is as open as the ocean.

SELF-WORTH
1. **Belief**: Everyone on earth is valuable, and carries within them a spark of divinity.
2. **Belief**: I have been blessed with many gifts.
3. **Belief**: If I don't use these gifts to help others, they will be taken away.

4. **Belief**: *If I don't live up to my personal standards, my self-worth is lessened.*

MY PLACE IN THE WORLD
1. **Belief**: *I'm here to learn, to grow, to enjoy, to appreciate, to love, and to do all the good that I can do.*
2. **Belief**: *I'm here to help the people I love get on with their purpose.*
3. **Belief**: *I wouldn't be as happy being anyone else. I fill my own crazy shoes perfectly.*
4. **Belief**: *Directly or indirectly, I'm going to make the world a happier place.*

4

EXPLORING AND EVALUATING YOUR BELIEFS

Because your beliefs create your life, it's in your best interest to explore and evaluate them carefully.

By listing your beliefs in Adventures 2 and 3, you have already discovered many of the attitudes that are shaping your life. Don't worry about the beliefs that escaped your first inspection. They will make themselves known as your ability for self-examination increases with practice.

Right now, you can begin identifying additional beliefs by paying careful attention to your thoughts, and by listening to the conversations you have with your self throughout the day. These thoughts and inner dialogues represent beliefs. Make note of them. Add them to your lists.

When you examine your beliefs with patience and an open mind, sooner or later you will prove to your satisfaction that what exists in your life existed *first* in your beliefs.

Exploring your beliefs explains much about your *now* self. You can trace them to discover how they have formed the person you know as your self. You can see where you will be going if you maintain your current beliefs. Evaluating your beliefs, one at a time, reveals both the excellent positive beliefs that produce the experiences you desire, and the limiting, negative beliefs that cause the experiences you want to change.

This chapter describes the different kinds of beliefs: principal and supporting, positive and negative, contradictory and outdated. In Adventure 4, you will use this information to better identify and understand your own belief system.

PRINCIPAL BELIEFS AND SUPPORTING BELIEFS

Principal beliefs represent your strongest ideas about your self, others, and the world. These are the basic attitudes that shape your life. The strength of these beliefs attract other ideas of a similar nature. Supporting beliefs reinforce your principal beliefs. They were attracted by these principal beliefs, and their power is derived from them.

Here are examples of both:

Principal Belief: I'm a healthy person.
Supporting Belief: I'm not susceptible to catching colds.

Principal Belief: I'm not a likable person.

Supporting Belief: My family doesn't really care about me.

Principal Belief: Life is to be enjoyed.

Supporting Belief: It's better to take the weekend off than to earn overtime working Sunday.

In each example, the principal belief is a powerful, major concept; the supporting belief backs it up. A principal belief is a magnetic force that draws many supporting beliefs. Once you identify a principal belief, you will more readily recognize the supporting ideas it has attracted. It's easy to understand why someone who believes, "I'm a healthy person," will also believe, "I'm not susceptible to catching colds." When you change a principal belief, the ideas that derived from that basic attitude can be quickly altered. The individual who changes the principal belief, "I'm not a likable person," will find it much easier to alter the supporting idea, "My family doesn't really care about me."

POSITIVE BELIEFS

Positive beliefs are those ideas that validate your basic goodness and worth. They promote health, happiness and well-being. They confirm your right to become the person you want to be, living the life you desire. Some examples:

- I am good.
- I deserve health, happiness, peace and prosperity.
- I am capable of creating everything I need and *want*.
- My relationships with others contribute to my personal happiness.
- Life is meant to be an exciting, joyful, creative learning experience.

Positive beliefs are easy to recognize. An examination of your belief system will undoubtedly reveal that your most successful and fulfilling experiences are in the areas where you have strong positive attitudes.

NEGATIVE BELIEFS

Negative beliefs are ideas that deny your basic goodness and value; they limit your potential for achievement, prosperity, health and happiness. They refute your right to become the person you want to be, living the life you desire. For example:

- I am bad.
- My life has no worth or purpose.
- I'm basically weak and unhealthy.
- Other people only want to bring me down.
- Life's a struggle.

Negative beliefs are often more difficult to recognize than positive beliefs. That's because we frequently mistake these limiting attitudes for "facts of life." But few, if any, of the negative beliefs we hold are unchangeable facts. Many of them were first accepted from others. Our experience may *seem* to validate a negative belief, but it was the belief that created the experience, not the experience that created the belief.

Shelley, a former student, is one of those people who mistook personal beliefs for facts: When asked to write a *factual* self-profile, she quickly scribbled, "I'm an unattractive woman of 25. . . . I'm a college graduate, but I guess I'm not very bright because I'm always making the wrong decisions. . . ."

Shelley whole-heartedly believed that her harsh self-appraisal was factual. As she put it, "I'm just telling it the way it is!" *In fact*, her description was a combination of facts and personal beliefs that she mistook for facts. Read Shelley's self-description again. Can you tell the difference between the facts and her personal beliefs?

The facts: Shelley is a woman; she was 25 years old at the time, and she is a college graduate.

Shelley's personal beliefs: She *believed* herself to be "unattractive," "not very bright," and "always making the wrong decisions."

First, Shelley had to distinguish her personal beliefs from the unalterable facts of life. Once that was accomplished, she examined her beliefs: "I'm unattractive...not very bright...always making the wrong decisions." Exploring these attitudes, she discovered that their *original* source was not to be found in her personal experience. Shelley remembered that she had first accepted these beliefs from a jealous older sister "who constantly put me down!"

After Shelley understood that her beliefs were not facts but negative ideas blindly accepted from a jealous sister, she began to change them. Eventually, Shelley re-created her self-image in a more positive light.

Some negative beliefs are so widely accepted as "facts" that they have become enshrined in cultural cliches. How many times have you heard one of the following "truisms"?

- It's a dog-eat-dog world.
- Money is the root of all evil.
- The rich get richer, and the poor get poorer.
- You can't fight city hall.
- You can't know happiness until you've known sorrow.
- You can't have everything.
- In life, everyone has a "cross" to bear.

Those bleak bromides are beliefs, not facts of life. Nonetheless, as long as we mistake them for facts, and they remain prevailing cultural attitudes, we will, en masse, create the "reality" of a dog-eat-dog world in which you can't have everything.

A negative belief is like a prison sentence: It severely restricts your freedom, limits your experience and condemns you to a life of hard labor in the area where the belief is held.

CONTRADICTORY BELIEFS

Contradictory beliefs are ideas that are directly opposed to other beliefs you accept. Because they represent conflicting attitudes about "reality," contradictory beliefs produce mixed results in the areas where they are held.

The person who believes, "I deserve the best things money can buy," and, "Money is the root of all evil," has contradictory beliefs. The woman who believes in a perfect Creator, yet believes herself to be a flawed creation, is holding contradictory beliefs. The husband who believes he should be faithful to his wife, but believes himself incapable of fidelity, has contradictory beliefs.

A belief held *without* contradiction, whether positive or negative, is a powerful creative force.

OUTDATED BELIEFS

An outdated belief is an idea that once worked for you, but now works against you. In other words, the belief has outlived its usefulness. If you suspect a belief of being outdated, re-examine and re-evaluate its impact on your life. Is it still creating experiences you want? If it isn't, the belief needs to be changed.

To take an extreme example, as a young child, you may have believed that you needed a parent to help you dress and tie your shoes. If you are 30 years old and still believe you need to be helped into your clothes, then you are holding an outdated belief. It was a valid belief when you were three; it's absurd at 30.

A more realistic example is the adult who still believes that he needs others to make decisions for him. Those others may be parents, friends, co-workers, a marriage partner or even an organization. As a child, this person was helped by having others guide his decision-making. In adulthood, this individual's personal growth is crippled by an outdated belief in his inability to make his own choices.

ADVENTURE 4

EXPLORING AND EVALUATING MY BELIEFS

Using the information in this chapter, you can determine the nature and category of your own personal beliefs.

STEP 1: Review your belief lists from Adventures 2 and 3. List any new beliefs, or new categories of beliefs, that you have discovered since completing those adventures.

STEP 2: Examine each belief on your lists individually, noting whether it is a principal belief (a basic attitude about life), or a supporting belief (an idea that reinforces a principal belief).

STEP 3: Evaluate each belief on your lists. Try to be objective. Is it positive or negative? Remember, a positive belief contributes to your health, happiness and well-being. A negative belief creates feelings of unworthiness, inadequacy, fear, loss and lack.

YOUR GUIDE FOR ADVENTURE 4

RALPH, 44 YEARS OLD:

I'm using Ralph's example in the "health" category as a model. You will be exploring and evaluating *all* the belief categories that you listed in Adventures 2 and 3, as well as any new categories of personal beliefs that you have since discovered.

HEALTH

1. **Belief**: *To a large extent, heredity determines your personal health. This is a principal belief. It is negative.*
2. **Belief**: *In the end, diet and exercise don't help much if you come from unhealthy "stock." This is a supporting belief. It is negative.*
3. **Belief**: *Both my parents died of cancer when they were in their 50's, so I probably will, too. Supporting belief: Negative.*
4. **Belief**: *I'm in great physical shape for a man my age—or any age. Principal belief: Positive.*
5. **Belief**: *I'm stronger than a lot of guys 20 years younger than me. Supporting belief: Positive.*
6. **Belief**: *Health decreases as your age increases. Principal belief: Negative.*
7. **Belief**: *I'm more likely to have health problems now than I was ten years ago. Supporting belief: Negative.*
8. **Belief**: *Basically, we have little control over our health. Principal belief: Negative.*

5

YOU *CAN* RE-CREATE YOUR SELF

With every chapter, you're learning more about your self. Exploring your lists in Adventure 4, you discovered additional beliefs that are shaping your life. Evaluating your lists, you identified your principal beliefs and the supporting beliefs that reinforce them; you distinguished the positive beliefs that create the experiences you want from the negative beliefs that produce unsatisfactory results.

Your challenge is clear: To re-create your self, to become the person you want to be, living the life you desire, you must change the negative and outdated beliefs that are creating the unsatisfactory conditions of your life.

If you already believe in your ability to change, then this chapter will reaffirm and strengthen that positive belief. If you're thinking, "People can't really change," this chapter will help you *change your beliefs* about your ability to make the changes you desire.

Consider this: Your beliefs create your life; therefore, you, and *only you*, control your life, forming your experiences in line with your belief system. Because you can examine and evaluate each belief, and decide whether or not you want to keep it, then it follows that you, and *only you*, can make the changes you desire, by discarding those beliefs that do not produce the desired results.

YOU CONTROL YOUR LIFE

You are the author of the "autobiography" you call your life. If you're unhappy with some of the "chapters," you can re-write them until you're satisfied. But first you must accept the fact that *you*, and not some "ghostwriter," are doing the writing.

Many people deny authorship of their life story. They may accept *some* responsibility for their experiences—but only up to a point. Beyond that point, they believe their life is out of their control. They claim that these uncontrollable "chapters" of their life are not written by them, but by some "collaborator." They call that collaborator by many names: God, the Fates, luck (both good and bad), karma, or the stars.

The truth is, you are the *sole* author of your life story.

You see, we live in an orderly universe: The sun rises in the east every morning and sets in the west every night; gravity is a consistent, not whimsical, force. We are a part of—not apart from—the universe's natural order. In other words, either we control our lives, or we don't. Either *nothing* is an accident, or *everything* is an accident.

Have you accepted responsibility for your life? Have you claimed the power and privilege to control your destiny? If you haven't, you're harboring a false belief about the way life works. You are surrendering self-responsibility to whatever outside forces you believe are in control.

TAKE MY POWER . . . PLEASE!

"Take my wife . . . please!" It's an old joke.

People seem equally eager to give away the power to control their life, and that's no joke. They find many ways to do it. "I'm a victim of my past," is a lament I hear frequently. When you accept this negative belief, you invest past experiences with an unnatural power. And you miss the point: You are meant to learn from the past, not be controlled by it.

Your purpose is to develop self-knowledge through experience, replacing the beliefs that limited past achievement with attitudes that will form a more successful future. Your power to create your life is in the present, and this power should be increased, not diminished, by what you've learned from past experiences—both good and bad. You aren't a victim of your past, unless you *believe* you are.

"I must have been *awful* in a past life, because I'm sure paying for it now!" It's amazing how often I hear this kind of self-indictment from people who consider themselves "spiritually aware." Even more dangerous than surrendering control of your life to past experiences is accepting the false belief that *past-life* transgressions are causing your present problems. If this is your belief, then you misunderstand the concept of karma.

Karma represents the sum total of your experiences. It indicates fortuitous directions for personal growth and education. Karma doesn't imply punishment, nor does it dictate current events. You aren't a cosmic prisoner serving time for the crimes of some past life you probably don't even remember. The universe doesn't judge and sentence anything or *anybody*. Karma doesn't infringe upon your free will. Your life isn't controlled by a karmic debt from this, or any, lifetime—unless you *believe* it is.

"I just can't control my temper! I'm always getting into arguments and fights, then later I feel terrible. But what can I do? *I'm Aries,* the Ram. Aries people are angry and stubborn, always 'butting heads' with others, especially other Aries." So moaned a friend who believed that his experiences were determined, now and forever, by a zodiacal sign.

A belief in astrology, as it is most commonly understood, can be another way of saying, "Take my power ... please!" But the belief that your life is charted by the positions and movements of heavenly bodies is just that—a *belief*, not a fact of life. Prove it for your self by opening a newspaper and reading your daily horoscope for a week, or by meeting one of the many Aries people who are peaceful and good-natured, not testy and quarrelsome. Your life is not controlled by the stars, unless you *believe* it is.

"My boyfriend's negativity is creating bad experiences in my life," confided a student. Five minutes earlier, she had laughed smugly, poking fun at people who blamed karma or the stars for their problems. Yet here she was blaming her bad experiences on her boyfriend, a mere mortal. "He's really powerful and strong-willed, like a Svengali," she continued. "I just can't resist doing whatever he asks."

If someone is controlling you, it's only because you have, on some level, willingly surrendered control. You have told that person, either verbally or mentally, "Take my power ... please!" Your life is not controlled by others, unless you believe it is.

To whom, or to what, are *you* saying, "Take my power ... please"? Have you ever said something like this: "God willing, I'll get that job," or "I'll get well, if it's God's will"? Your life is no more controlled by God than by any other external force. If you believe in a Supreme Being, then understand: It is God's will for you to use the *free will* that He gave you. To do otherwise is to throw that precious gift back in His face. When you believe that God manipulates and controls you, then you are reducing the Supreme Being to little more than a Cosmic Buttinsky. Your life isn't controlled by a meddlesome, punishing God unless you *believe* it is.

Once again, you and *you alone* have the power, the privilege and the responsibility to control your life. Are you willing to accept control? Or do you feel the need to burden God, or some other external force, with a responsibility that is naturally your own?

YOU CAN CHANGE YOUR SELF

Do you believe the cultural cliche, "You can't teach an old dog new tricks?" One of the most negative and limiting attitudes of all is the belief that you can't change. If you believe you must accept your problems, then that attitude alone can prevent you from solving them.

You *can* re-create your self. If your current beliefs are not contributing to your well-being, then you can change them, and by so doing, change your life. Once you understand that you, and *only you* control your life, then it follows that you, and *only you* can change it.

CHANGE IS A NATURAL PROCESS

The inability to change is self-inflicted, and not based on any natural law. It's only when you believe your self incapable of change that you find it extremely difficult, or impossible. But change is the most *natural* process in the world. The proof is all around you: Look at the weather, the seasons, the flowers and trees. Change is the natural order.

The proof is *within* you, too. Your body changes constantly. Old cells die and are replaced by new ones. The body you have now is literally not the same body you had seven years ago. Nor is your mind static and unchangeable. The unpredictability of your own thoughts should make this clear. Try concentrating on a single idea without allowing the focus of your attention to be changed by an unrelated thought. This experiment will quickly prove that change is not only possible, it's unstoppable!

Your potential for change is far greater than you realize. You can create, and re-create, your self for as long as you are alive. You start by acknowledging your natural ability to change. Then you commit your self to making the changes you desire. You initiate change by exploring and evaluating, then accepting or rejecting, attitudes beyond the limits of your current philosophies and prejudices. Finally, you act upon your new beliefs, thereby allowing them to create new life experiences.

CHANGE IS NOTHING TO FEAR

Many people fear change. They are afraid of the unknown. They fear that their attempt to change will result in failure. You may be one of these people.

Change is nothing to fear. It is a gradual process. The unknown is slowly revealed as the change occurs. The process progresses at a pace that is comfortable and safe. By the time the change is completed, what was formerly unknown has become known and familiar.

There is no reason to fear that your attempt to change will meet with failure. *Re-Creating Your Self* doesn't mean that you must transform your life from "unsatisfactory" to "perfect." Changing any aspect of your life from "unsatis-factory" to "better" qualifies as a success. Self-improvement, no matter how small you believe it to be, confirms your natural ability to change; it increases your confidence. Your next attempt to change will meet with even greater success.

ADVENTURE 5

MY PERSONAL ABILITY TO CHANGE

Prove your natural ability for change by listing the negative beliefs that you have changed in the past. First, list each negative belief that you originally held. From whom did you first accept it? What negative experiences did the belief create? Next, write down the positive belief that replaced it. When did you change the belief? How did you change it? How has the new belief improved your experiences?

The following example, provided by your guide, Denise, may help you remember some of your own changed beliefs.

YOUR GUIDE FOR ADVENTURE 5

DENISE, 29 YEARS OLD:

Old, negative belief: I am physically weak and susceptible to illness. Because I was born premature and underweight, my mother believed I was frail, and I accepted that belief from her. Consequently, I experienced what must have been one of the unhealthiest childhoods on record: I had all the so-called childhood diseases, and a lot of "adult" diseases, too.

New, positive belief: I am physically strong and healthy. I began changing my negative attitude after I went off to college. Away from my mother's constant reminders, I forgot to believe I was sickly. What's more, my college friends were always saying that I looked "disgustingly healthy" and full of energy. As my attitude changed, so did my experiences: I no longer believed I'd catch pneumonia by going outside without a sweater, and I didn't. In the last ten years, I haven't had anything more serious than a short bout with the flu.

Old, negative belief: Someone else's success makes it more difficult for me to succeed. I honestly don't remember where I picked up this idea, but I used to believe there was only so much success to go around, and someone else's success took something away from my chance of succeeding. In school, I was jealous of my classmates' accomplishments. I even begrudged the achievements of my family and friends. News of someone's else's success drained my energy, made me sick with envy.

New, positive belief: I am inspired by the success of others. Again, college was the turning point. I noticed how my roommate Darlene was genuinely happy whenever a friend scored a success. I found this irritating. I called her a "goody-two shoes." But Darlene didn't believe that the success of others diminished her own chances. On the contrary, the achievement of others inspired her. Ever so slowly, I began accepting Darlene's point of view. Today, I can honestly say that I feel energized, not enervated, when a friend or co-worker succeeds.

Old, negative belief: To succeed in my carreer, I have to work longer and harder than anyone else. I first accepted this belief from my father, a world-class workaholic. He stayed at the office later than anyone but still brought work home. He rarely took off weekends. I never remember him taking more than a one-week vacation. He believed this was necessary for success in a highly competitive world. Until recently, I followed in his weary footsteps. But all work and no play made me an unhappy, exhausted and dull girl. Making things worse, I wasn't advancing any faster in my career than my friends who insisted on lots of leisure time and regular vacations.

New, positive belief: It's not the hours I put into my work, it's the work I put into my hours. I heard this from a friend, and *when she explained her philosophy, it did make sense. I'm still working at more fully accepting this new belief, but I'm already experiencing the beneficial results. I've stopped taking work home, and I don't work on weekends. I'm having fun. I'm trying new things, like this course. I'm more relaxed. These days, I go to work feeling full of energy, not tired. I'm happy to be there, not resentful. I'm a more pleasant person to work with. And, I swear, I accomplish in one hour what it took me two hours to do when I believed I was a "workhorse."*

6

YOU ARE *MORE* THAN YOU KNOW

You are more than you think you are. The person you call *your self* is only part of a more expansive self. When you get to know this expansive self, you will discover that your personal consciousness is greater and more flexible than you imagined. You will stop underestimating your potential. Self-limiting attitudes will dissolve. You will *know* that you have *within* you everything you need to become the person you want to be, living the life you desire.

Your expansive self is a powerhouse of creativity with infinite potential, but you can't fully use its godlike power if you're unaware of its existence. Your goal, then, is not to expand your consciousness but to expand your *knowledge* of the expansive consciousness you already have.

Limiting your knowledge of your expansive self are the false beliefs you have accepted about personhood in general, and about your self in particular. I'm talking about philosophies that deny the basic goodness, value and purpose of the individual, attitudes that discourage individuality and encourage homogenization, beliefs that cause you to label your self and thus limit your experiences.

Unfortunately, many of these self-limiting beliefs are taught to us by society's most powerful and authoritative organizations. Tragically, these lessons in personal limitation are among our earliest and most influential memories. If we continue to allow others to define our personal boundaries, then we will certainly overlook our potential beyond those boundaries.

To develop a broader knowledge of your expansive self, you must first reject the negative beliefs that diminish and degrade the very nature of selfhood. You can do this by: (1) learning to trust and value your self, (2) acknowledging and expressing your individuality, and, (3) peeling off the "labels" that limit your experiences.

TRUST AND VALUE YOUR SELF

You are inherently good and trustworthy; you are valuable, and you have purpose. These are basic qualities of selfhood, but, sadly, the world is often anxious to deny your goodness and worth. We are living in a time when a belief in the basic goodness of the individual has been sharply discounted, if

not totally discarded—an era when the beauty and inno-
cence of selfhood have been replaced by the belief that we
are born guilty and flawed.

When asked to trace the source of their belief in a
flawed, untrustworthy self, many students discover that
they first accepted these ideas during early childhood from
a strong source of authority, frequently a religious organization. Mary's remarks are typical:

"I was told that I was *born* sinful. Apparently, God
hadn't forgiven me for the transgressions of my *original*
ancestors. Even as a young child, I thought this was carrying the concept of guilt by association to an absurd
extreme, not worthy of *any* God, much less the perfect God
my religion promoted. Besides, wasn't erring supposed to
be human and forgiving Divine?

"I was taught that the Son of God died for *my* sins!
'What sins?' I asked myself. Was just *existing* sinful in itself?
Was the very state of *being* a damnable one? What kind of
sadistic God would demand His Son's blood to 'save' the
species He had created? And what kind of masochistic Son
would comply with such a morbid, tyrannical demand?

"My religion told me that my body was dirty, my mind
was the devil's playground. Accepting these beliefs, even in
part, made my life a hell on earth. Later, *I* ex-communi-
cated my church, but the brainwashing lingered on. Too
often, I have to remind myself that I am basically good and
trustworthy."

Unfortunately, I hear variations of Mary's story with
alarming frequency. It sometimes seems that the First
Commandment of many religions is, "Thou Shalt Not Trust
Thy Self!" Consequently, these powerful organizations
have been more successful at limiting man's feelings of self-
trust and self-value than at expanding them.

Many religions define selfhood as essentially sinful
and untrustworthy. Humankind is perceived as the one
flawed, undeserving species in an otherwise good and

orderly universe. Earth life is viewed as "a valley of sorrow," not the joyous opportunity for creativity it is meant to be. Even the more "enlightened" Eastern creeds consider physical life a second-rate existence, something to be patiently endured until the spirit is free to assume residence on a superior plane.

But if you believe that the physical world is a ghetto, then you will create a shabby life. When you accept a religion's belief that selfhood is by nature sinful and untrustworthy, then you must reject your basic goodness and value; you must deny your right to personal happiness.

The untrustworthy nature of selfhood taught by many religions glaringly contradicts religion's belief in a perfect God. Ultimately, how can you trust in a perfect God if you can't trust your self, the creation of that Perfection?

Other students trace their lack of self-trust and self-value to beliefs they have accepted from the modern sciences, which have become "religions" in their own right. Recalls Jordy, another student of mine, "My parents were atheists. Science was their god. Mine too, I guess. The problem is, science told me the world, and everything in it, was an accident. *I* was an accident. So, how could I trust myself ... I mean, *how can you trust an accident?* I felt worthless ... pointless ... impotent. I was afraid *another* accident might suddenly destroy the world as capriciously as it had created it."

Modern science's belief in selfhood as an accidental, haphazard phenomenon denies the individual's value as effectively as religion's belief in a sinful, untrustworthy self. Other scientific beliefs only make matters worse:

Freudians believe that selfhood is basically savage, amoral and egocentric. They say the inner self, or unconscious mind, is fearsome and depraved, not unlike religion's devil. The individual's deepest feelings are suspect; his desires are beyond self-comprehension. Freudians believe that deep self-analysis is, at best, a risky business. They say the individual needs a psychoanalyst to gain self-understanding, the way religion claims he needs the church in order to be saved. (In fact, what the individual really needs to be saved from are these negative beliefs.)

About the same time Freud first told us not to trust our minds, the medical sciences were warning us not to depend on our bodies. Suddenly, the magnificent physical organism—the temple of our expansive consciousness—which *automatically* performs countless life-sustaining functions, was believed to be incapable of keeping its own house in healthy order.

Today you are blitzed by so-called public service announcements insisting that, without constant examination, your body will eventually betray you. As if that weren't bad enough, advertisers use television, radio, newspapers, magazines and billboards to convince you that your body can't properly perform such basic, natural functions as digesting food or eliminating it without their products.

Considering the negative, limiting beliefs we have accepted about ourselves, it's no surprise that many people have lost their sense of goodness, self-trust, value and purpose.

But you need to remember that the beliefs of any organization, no matter how much authority it possesses, are simply widely accepted theories, not necessarily facts of life. These beliefs are subject to change. Old "facts" are regularly replaced by new ones. Until the 1960s, tens of millions of Roman Catholics believed that the punishment for eating a hamburger on Friday could be eternal damnation. In an earlier time, the scientific community believed the earth was flat.

Also, before accepting any organizational beliefs, remember this: *All* organizations, be they religious, scientific, political, business, or fraternal, have a vested interest in cultivating your dependency on their philosophies. Quite simply, people can live without organizations, but organizations die without people. To survive, an organization must convince you that you need something that only it can provide.

Any organization that admits, "You don't need the organization. *Within* you is everything you need to live successfully," is, in effect, signing its own death warrant.

Life puts you in a one-on-one encounter with your self and the world. To win the game of life, it is necessary to trust and value your self. Don't let anyone, or any organization, define your personal goodness and value. The nature of selfhood is best known *directly* through you, the individual who experiences it, and not through any organization.

EXPLORE AND EXPRESS YOUR INDIVIDUALITY

Being an individual in a society that encourages homogenization is difficult, but you must explore and express your individuality in order to discover your expansive self. Aware of your special talents and eccentricities, you may downplay these abilities because you fear your own uniqueness. You may have been taught that personal originality is queer, eccentricity is bizarre. At home, at school, at work, and at play, you are encouraged to "fit in," to become "one of the gang." But you aren't "one of the gang." You are an *individual*. When you pretend to be less than you are, your perception of selfhood shrinks and, along with it, your potential for happiness.

When you express your individuality, self-knowledge increases, and so do your accomplishments. You help your self, and you inspire others. Personal eccentricities are frequently responsible for humankind's most outstanding achievements in philosophy, the arts and sciences. In fact, without individual expression, the human race would cease to develop. Imagine the world if Buddha and Christ, Mozart and Lennon, Michelangelo and Picasso, had bowed to societal pressure to be "one of the gang," to become standardized and homogenized.

You can reject all societal encouragement to become standardized, a "regular" Joe or Jane. The individual is by nature an *irregular* phenomenon. You can put aside all cultural concepts of the average person, the norm, the model this-or-that. These are merely abstract ideas; you are flesh and blood, life-carrying *reality.*

Take pride in your individuality; respect the individuality of others. Appreciate and cultivate your special abilities. Rejoice in the knowledge that you are unique and, in so doing, you will come to better know your expansive self.

PEEL OFF THE "LABELS"

Your expansive self is buried beneath the "labels" you have accepted as defining your self. For example, perhaps you think of your self primarily in terms of your sex. By labeling your self a man or a woman rather than a person, you limit self-expression, restricting your experiences to those that you and society consider appropriate for your sex.

Selfhood continues to shrink with each pigeonhole accepted: If you think of your self primarily as a man, and then attach the ethnic label Mexican-American, you further limit your experiences to those deemed acceptable for a Mexican-American man.

How many limiting "labels" have you attached to your self? Peel them off and discover a more expansive self.

ADVENTURE 6

MY BELIEFS ABOUT THE NATURE OF SELFHOOD

STEP 1: To your belief lists, add your beliefs about:

> My basic goodness
> My ability to trust my self
> My personal value.

If your lists reveal that you believe your self to be basically good, trustworthy and valuable, move on to Step 2. If you believe your self to be basically bad, untrustworthy, or valueless, then write why you feel this way. Were these negative beliefs first accepted from others, or were they the result of your personal experiences? Examine objectively everything you have written. Remember, these are your current beliefs about your self and not necessarily facts of life. These beliefs can be changed.

STEP 2: How comfortable are you with your self? List your beliefs about individuality. Include your attitude about expressing your own special talents, eccentricities and quirks. How do you feel when others express theirs?

YOUR GUIDE FOR ADVENTURE 6

Georgia, your guide for Adventure 3, also provides the example for this adventure.

STEP 1

MY BASIC GOODNESS
1. *Belief*: *I try harder to be good than anyone I know.*
2. *Belief*: *If I have to try, then it doesn't come naturally; therefore I am not naturally, or basically, good.*
3. *Belief*: *Basic goodness involves supreme simplicity.*
4. *Belief*: *I am too complicated to be truly good.*
5. *Belief*: *Basic goodness involves being secure—it is hard to be good to others if you aren't good to yourself.*
6. *Belief*: *I am rotten to myself.*
7. *Belief*: *Basic goodness is something you're born with. I was given long eyelashes instead.*

MY ABILITY TO TRUST MYSELF
1. *Belief*: *I can be trusted never to let anyone else down.*
2. *Belief*: *I let myself down constantly.*
3. *Belief*: *My advice to others is brilliantly trustworthy.*
4. *Belief*: *I can't trust the advice I give myself.*

MY PERSONAL VALUE
1. *Belief*: *When I do something to deserve it, I'm valuable.*
2. *Belief*: *When I don't, I'm not.*
3. *Belief*: *My value in my own eyes isn't lessened by anyone else's low opinion of me—unless it's the opinion of someone I love. Then I'm sunk.*

WHY I FEEL THIS WAY
Being human isn't good enough for me; I long to be superhuman and utterly wonderful. I grew up with "Little

Women" as my bible, and I totally accepted the saintly value-system of that book's fictitious family.

Also, I have actually met one or two non-fictitious people who are almost totally good and trustworthy; so I know it is possible. And if it's possible, I'm going to keep trying.

Lastly, I want to be always balanced, always strong, always wise, always unselfish—and when I'm unbalanced, weak, silly and egocentric, it seems that I'm betraying all of my ideals.

WHERE MY BELIEFS CAME FROM

These beliefs about my goodness, trustworthiness and personal value weren't accepted from others. They are of my own creation. In fact, most people I know like and love me; they believe that I am good, trustworthy and valuable. But I suspect they like me for my strengths, not my weaknesses, and so I'm terrified of showing any weakness, for fear the love will stop.

STEP 2:

INDIVIDUALITY

1. **Belief:** I am a flaming, ardent, rampant, individualist. "Weird, and proud of it!" has always been my motto.
2. **Belief:** Individuality is something to be cherished and nurtured and shouted from the rooftops.
3. **Belief:** The death of someone's individuality is like the death of Bambi's mother.
4. **Belief:** Alone or with others, I am usually comfortable expressing my individuality.
5. **Belief:** There are times when I stop myself from expressing the true extent of my individuality.
6. **Belief:** I am delighted to see others express their individuality. I encourage them to do so.
7. **Belief:** There are times when I am embarrassed by the method a person chooses for expressing individuality. This is especially true if the form of expression is in any way vulgar or sexual.

7

PLANNING YOUR *NEW* SELF

This chapter provides you with a matchless opportunity for creativity. It is your chance to design the blueprint for your *new* self—the person you want to become. This may be the first time you have claimed the power and the privilege to create your self.

Designing your blueprint for personal change is a determining step in transforming your self from *other*-created to *self*-created. Before taking that important step, let's recap the basic principles of *Re-Creating Your Self*.

You have the power, the privilege—and the responsibility—to become the person you want to be, living the life you desire. You alone create your life. You are not controlled by *any* outside forces, and that includes God. Your original source, or God, is a creative force, not a manipulative one. Free will is your birthright. Your life is what *you* make it.

You create your life in line with your beliefs. This is not just my opinion. Throughout the ages, many of humankind's greatest teachers, Buddha and Christ among them, have taught this dynamic principle: Your beliefs create your reality. That's how life works; it's what makes things happen.

Earth is a school. You are a student. You attend this school to learn how the energy of your mental beliefs eventually forms physical matter. In Schoolhouse Earth (and in most dictionaries), a belief is defined as any idea you accept as being true.

The person you are *now*, with the experiences you call your own, was created largely by beliefs you first acquired from others. Many of "your" ideas about reality were blindly accepted from the people who most influenced your childhood, rather than being gained through your personal experience. These people, along with the prevalent cultural attitudes of the times, largely defined reality for you. They defined your concepts of selfhood and the world.

Some of the beliefs you accepted from others were negative. It follows that when you create your life with negative beliefs, you get negative results. A successful life is the product of a positive belief system that confirms your basic goodness and value and promotes personal achievement, creativity and well-being.

You can re-create your self, becoming the person you want to be, living the life you desire, by replacing your negative beliefs with positive beliefs. The first step is to *identify* your beliefs. You must also learn the difference between personal beliefs and the unalterable facts of life. Then examining and evaluating your beliefs one at a time will reveal the positive beliefs that create your successful experiences, and the negative and outdated beliefs that limit your success.

You *can* change negative and outdated beliefs. The inability to change is self-inflicted, and not based on any universal law. *Change is a natural process.* For as long as you're alive, it's never too late, or too early, to change.

Your ability to re-create your self—to make the changes you desire—increases as you learn more about the enormous potential and creativity *within* you. Discover the excellence and expansiveness of selfhood by learning to trust your self, and by exploring and expressing your individuality, free of the "labels" and pigeonholes that limit personal experience.

YOUR GREATER SELF-UNDERSTANDING

Through your exploration of the first six Inner Space Adventures, you have already achieved a greater self-understanding.

Congratulate your self on all you have learned.

You have defined your *now* self for your self. You have identified your good and bad qualities, your current abilities and limitations, what makes you happy, and what makes you sad and angry.

You have identified many of the beliefs that create your life, and you have traced the sources of those beliefs, finding that many of them were first accepted from *others*, without your careful scrutiny.

You have examined and evaluated your beliefs distinguishing the principal from the supporting, the positive from the negative.

You have proved your ability to change by listing the

negative beliefs you have already discarded.

You have analyzed your self, revealing your current ability to trust your self, and to express your individuality.

These accomplishments are impressive, and this greater self-understanding will help you to re-create your self.

YOUR *NEW* SELF

It's time to start planning your *new* self: Begin by reviewing your belief system. That includes *all* the beliefs you listed in the first six adventures. Be sure to re-read the self-description you wrote for Adventure 1. It, too, represents your beliefs about who you are. Do you still agree with your previous evaluations? In other words, upon review, does a belief that you labeled *supporting* now appear to be *principal*? Does a belief you first evaluated as *positive* now seem to be *negative*, or *outdated*? Make changes as necessary.

During this review, you may identify additional beliefs, maybe even entirely new categories of beliefs. From whom did you first accept these beliefs? Are they principal or supporting? Positive or negative? Do they represent outdated attitudes? Update your lists to include the new information. After completing your review, pat your self on the back for the positive beliefs contained on your lists.

Now, turn your attention to the beliefs you labeled negative and outdated. Have you begun to change any of these limiting attitudes since first identifying them? If the answer is yes, then you are well on your way to *Re-Creating Your Self*.

If the answer is no, don't be discouraged. The very fact that you have identified beliefs that need changing represents progress. And give your self credit for having the courage to accept responsibility for your actions.

In either case, your goal is to discard the remaining negative beliefs and outdated attitudes. This means rejecting all the philosophies that contradict your basic goodness and value, all the ideas that limit your potential for achievement, prosperity, health and happiness—quite simply, all the beliefs that are keeping you from becoming the person you want to be, living the life you desire.

ADVENTURE 7

MY BLUEPRINT FOR PERSONAL CHANGE

Design the blueprint for your *new* self, the person you want to become. Be generous with your self. Remember, there are few, if any, unsatisfactory aspects of your life that can't be changed.

STEP 1: Make a categorical list of the negative and outdated beliefs that you want to discard, leaving plenty of space after each belief to complete Steps 2 thru 4. Remind your self that this list represents your personal beliefs, and not unchangeable facts of life. For example, *believing*, "I'm unlikable," is much different than *being* unlikable in fact.

STEP 2: Examine these beliefs one at a time. Ask your self, "Why do I accept this limiting attitude? Write down your reasons.

STEP 3: In each case, write an *objective evaluation* of your reasons.

STEP 4: Write the new, positive belief that you want to replace the old, negative one.

YOUR GUIDE FOR ADVENTURE 7

During our first meeting, Lee blurted, "I'm trying to find a reason to go on living." Lee had health, financial security, a beautiful home and good friends. But none of that mattered to him. A year before, he had lost his wife to cancer. Making matters worse, he had become disenchanted and bored with his work. A great marriage and an exciting career had been Lee's reasons for living, and now they were gone. He believed personal happiness and fulfillment were impossible.

After completing the first six Inner Space Adventures, Lee was more hopeful about his potential for happiness. He came to understand that for him *Re-Creating Your Self* meant changing negative attitudes in three major categories: relationships, aging and career.

You will have your own number of categories of beliefs that need re-creating. Lee's adventure provides a format you can use for designing your own blueprint.

LEE, 48 YEARS OLD:

RELATIONSHIPS
1. ***Negative belief***: *I will never find happiness with another woman.*
2. ***Reasons for my belief***: *Betty was my high school sweetheart, my one and only love. We couldn't have children, so we built our lives around each other. I've never loved any human being as much as I loved Betty. No one has ever made me as happy. No one has ever cared so much about me. Betty was my wife, my best friend, my little girl and, sometimes, my mother. No one can replace her.*

3. ***Objective evaluation of my belief***: *I understand that (1) I'm still mourning Betty, (2) I'm feeling sorry for myself, (3) I'm feeling guilty for surviving my wife.*

    This is difficult for me to say, but because you insist that I be objective, I admit that it's possible I could be happy with another woman, though I'm not ready for that yet. That doesn't mean another woman could replace Betty, but I might be able to find a woman with qualities of her own that I would find lovable and appealing.

4. ***New belief***: *When I'm ready, I can have a relationship, or even a second marriage, that will be happy and meaningful.*

AGING

1. ***Negative belief***: *At 48, I'm at least thirteen years too old to start thinking about a new career.*
2. ***Reasons for my belief***: *It's just a fact of life. These days, you're over-the-hill at 35, at least where starting a new career is concerned.*
3. ***Objective evaluation of my belief***: *Ooops! I think this is an example of mistaking a culturally prevalent attitude for a fact of life. I suppose there are a lot of people who successfully start a new career, or even go back to school to learn one, during middle age. In fact, I know three people who have done this.*
4. ***New belief***: *My ability to make successful changes doesn't decrease with age, and that includes my ability to change careers.*

CAREER

1. ***Negative belief***: *There's really nothing more for me to learn about the real estate business.*
2. ***Reasons for my belief***: *I'm bored. I've been in the business for 26 years. There are no more surprises.*
3. ***Objective evaluation of my belief***: *All right, maybe it's not the business. Maybe it's me. Maybe I have become boring. After all these years, I've developed a know-it-all attitude.*

4. **New belief**: *My career can become exciting and challenging again. There is always something new to learn about any business.*

When completed, Adventure 7 becomes your blueprint for *Re-Creating Your Self*. Like everything else in life, your blueprint is subject to change. Feel free to make additions as you discover other beliefs that need altering.

Now you may be wondering, "Exactly *how* am I going to make the changes I've described in my blueprint?" The answer: The greater self-understanding that you now possess will help you accept your new beliefs. Additional assistance will be provided by the powerful tools for change described in Part Two.

PART TWO

CHANGING YOUR SELF: HOW TO DO IT

8

THINKING FOR YOUR SELF

One of the most essential tools for change is thinking for your self. To successfully accept the new, positive beliefs in your blueprint, you need to do your own thinking, unfettered by the attitudes of others.

Now, you may *think* that thinking for your self is the obvious, natural thing to do, and it is. But how often do you really do it? Answer that question for your self by noting how many of the beliefs on your lists were first acquired from others.

Remember, you became *other*-created by *not* thinking for your self, by allowing the important individuals and organizations from your childhood to define your reality according to their beliefs and the culturally prevalent attitudes of the time. From the start, you were taught to depend upon others to distinguish right from wrong, truth from fiction. You were rewarded for mechanically reciting beliefs—a parental dictum, a catechism, a school policy— accepted from an authority figure. You were sometimes scolded, or even punished, for questioning authority. Consequently, you came to believe that allowing others to think for you was good; it brought approval and reward.

Little wonder many of us go through life arbitrarily accumulating attitudes from others, even when those beliefs are limiting and defeating. It may seldom occur to us to seriously question the value of these ideas because we have been programmed to unthinkingly accept the "wisdom" of others, especially if those others are in a position of authority.

To re-create your self, you must learn to think for your self. You also need to recognize when you aren't doing your own thinking. You can begin by understanding that there is a major difference between being *told* things and *knowing* them for your self. When you're *told* something, the information comes to you from an outside source; *knowledge* comes from within, through personal experience. Being told something is no substitute for knowledge, and knowledge can be achieved only by thinking for your self.

To think for your self, put aside the attitudes and biases of others, as well as your own personal prejudices and previous programming. Then, with an open mind, examine and evaluate the new, positive beliefs contained in your blueprint. Accept or reject, re-think and revise, these new beliefs only after you have analyzed their validity and value for your self.

Apply this same kind of careful self-analysis to all the new ideas coming your way from outside sources, including your current teachers and counselors. Obviously, you don't want to collect new negative beliefs even as you're trying to discard the old ones.

TEACHERS

Wanting a happier, more fulfilling life, we all seek out teachers to help us. Sometimes the teacher is an individual or an organization; other times, the teacher comes in the form of a life-change seminar, or even a self-help book, such as this one. The teacher may be a loved one, or a stranger recommended by a friend. Make sure that your teachers are allowing you to think for your self.

Here are some guidelines to consider when looking for a good teacher.

Look for:

- teachers who guide, and do not command, their students.
- teachers who treat students in a loving and respectful manner.
- teachers who acknowledge your goodness and emphasize the positive qualities you already possess.
- teachers who practice what they preach.
- teachers willing to tailor their guidance to fit the needs of individual students.
- teachers who will not allow students to idolize them.
- teachers who let you know that your best teacher is the one within you.

Beware of:

- teachers who say your life will be a miserable failure without their help.
- teachers who claim to have a "copyright" on truth.
- teachers who want to control you.
- teachers who cultivate your dependency on them.
- teachers who want you to accept their beliefs on faith.
- teachers who want you to surrender your will to their own, or to their god's will.
- teachers who tell you that you are sinful, or bad.
- teachers who are egocentric, greedy or power-hungry.
- teachers who claim self-perfection.

Apply these guidelines, as well as your own standards, to your current teachers. How do they measure up? An objective evaluation of your teachers can be difficult, especially if they are loved ones, or organizations you have long held sacred. But it's important to periodically review the individuals, institutions and philosophies you turn to for guidance.

SELF-KNOWLEDGE IS YOUR PERSONAL SAVIOR

Many people, conditioned to look to others for answers, turn to an individual, an organization, or God for help and salvation. They place the burden of their hopes, their dreams and their fears on that person, that institution or that Savior.

In reality, self-knowledge is your only personal savior. There is nothing new, revolutionary or blasphemous about that statement. Humankind's greatest teachers, Jesus among them, have taught that, "The kingdom of God is within you." Your personal salvation is not to be found externally. It is not found by turning to another individual, an organization, or even a god. It is literally *within you.*

Salvation is the internal transformation of your consciousness into a state of self-realization. When you become a disciple of your own mind, you come to know both your self and your source, or God. This self-realization is your salvation, and it can be achieved only through the self-knowledge that comes with personal experience.

SIN IS CAUSED BY IGNORANCE

Sin is commonly defined as an offense against God, a violation of nature or our fellow man. It is ignorance, and not any inborn evil, that causes us to sin—to violate the laws of God and nature. No savior has to die for our sins (ignorance). We don't need to suffer for our sins (ignorance)—nor do we need to be punished for our sins (ignorance). Those ancient ideas are unenlightened and masochistic. Humankind has spent thousands of years living with those self-destructive beliefs, and neither man nor the world is better for it.

Our challenge is to replace the darkness of ignorance with the light of knowledge. We begin by accepting this challenge, rather than casting the burden for our redemption upon the shoulders of some "savior."

DEVELOP "SALES RESISTANCE"

There are many reasons why people want to think for you. Sometimes people are well-intentioned, though misguided. Other times, their motives are self-serving.

Regardless of the intent, whenever someone tries to think for you, that person is, in effect, trying to sell you something. That "something" may be a mouthwash, a political ideology, a relationship or a ticket to heaven. Whatever the product, the "salesperson's" job is made easier when you unthinkingly accept his beliefs. His efforts are further helped by the conditioning that causes you to look outside your self for answers. The salesperson often preys upon your ignorance, fears and guilt. He may not be above threatening you with everything from halitosis to hellfire in order to sell you a product.

You must learn to recognize when someone is trying to sell you something—when someone is trying to think for you—and develop sales resistance. Do you really need, or want, what he is selling? Decide for your self. Remember, no one has the power to think for you unless you give him the power.

You are living in a fool's paradise if you believe that you can achieve happiness by allowing others to think for you. There is really no way to absolve your self of the responsibility for your own success. Looking to others for the answers to your problems doesn't build a strong foundation for personal growth; it can only add to your fears, insecurities and feelings of inadequacy.

ALLOW OTHERS TO THINK FOR THEMSELVES

In addition to thinking for your self, and learning to recognize when you aren't, you must allow others to think for themselves, and recognize when you're trying to think for them.

Do you sometimes believe that you know what's best for someone? If so, understand that it isn't your right, or your responsibility, to think for someone else. Whenever you are about to tell a friend, "Take my word for it. Don't do that. It'll only bring you heartache," you may be hindering, not helping, your friend. Like you, the people in your life are here to gain self-knowledge through personal experience. They aren't meant to live according to the advice of others, and that includes your own invaluable advice.

Parents, it is your right and responsibility to guide your young children, to give them a basic orientation to life, to provide a direction for personal growth. However, some of you feel compelled to "call the shots" long after your children have matured. You are convinced that you know the career, the spouse, the friends, the house, the lifestyle, that will best serve your offspring. If you are one of these parents, learn to let go. Accept responsibility for creating your own happiness, and give your children the same opportunity. Besides, if your own beliefs have produced an exemplary lifestyle, then your children will learn from your example, and they won't need your unsolicited advice.

Once again, each individual needs to think for himself, to gain self-knowledge through first-hand experience, and not to live according to hand-me-down beliefs.

I'm going to let Buddha have the last word on thinking for your self:

> *Believe nothing because a wise man said it,*
> *Believe nothing because it is generally held,*
> *Believe nothing because it is written,*
> *Believe nothing because it is said to be divine,*
> *Believe nothing because someone else believes it,*
> *But believe only what you yourself judge to be true.*

ADVENTURE 8

THINKING FOR MY SELF

STEP 1: Do you still allow others to think for you? List the sources from which you currently accept new beliefs on faith, without your own careful self-analysis. Include scientific, religious, spiritual, political, business and social organizations, as well as friends, lovers, family, co-workers and teachers.

STEP 2: Do you try to think for others? Consider your children, spouse, friends, students, co-workers and the others in your life. Make a list of those for whom you try to think.

9

FALLING IN LOVE WITH YOUR SELF

Self-love is an indispensable tool for *Re-Creating Your Self*. When you love your self, you can create the best that life has to offer, because you know you deserve the best. When you don't love your self, you sabotage your heart's desires as automatically as you breathe, because you believe your self to be undeserving.

If you don't love your self now, then you must fall in love with your self before you can fully accept your positive new beliefs. If you do love your self, learning to love your self *more* will make it easier for you to become the person you want to be, living the life you desire.

NATURAL SELF-LOVE

In suggesting that you fall in love with your self, I am not encouraging conceit, narcissism, egocentricity, selfishness or any of the negative traits commonly associated with the concept of self-love.

When Christ advised, "...thou shalt love thy neighbor as thy self," he was taking a natural self-love for granted.

Natural self-love is the respectful acknowledgment of your personal goodness, value and originality. It includes a basic caring, interest and affection for your self. It means knowing that you have a right to be alive, and that you matter. Unlike narcissism and egocentricity, natural self-love includes the recognition that all other beings are worthwhile, important and unique; they have a right to be here, they matter.

This kind of self-love is a basic tool for successful living, but possessing it can't be taken for granted. Loving your self is difficult in a world that has accepted so many negative beliefs about the nature of selfhood. I have already mentioned some of these philosophies in Chapter 6: Religion's belief that selfhood is sinful, science's theory that selfhood is amoral and accidental, the beliefs that the individual is little more than a tool of society or the state.

ROMANCING YOUR SELF

If you don't possess a natural self-love now, then you must

begin to "court" your self. Learning to trust your self and express your individuality, as described in Chapter 6, are excellent starting points. Adopting the following attitudes will also help:

Fall in love with your self by seeing your self in the best possible light. Appreciate the good qualities you have *now*. Be excited and challenged by your potential for further growth and accomplishment. Don't dwell on your short-comings. This doesn't mean that you should ignore per-sonal flaws, but you shouldn't dislike or hate your self for them, either. You can learn from your flaws if you allow them to point the way toward future accomplishment. Viewed in this manner, flaws actually promote personal growth by indicating gaps in your development.

Fall in love with your self by refusing to compare your self to others. Don't measure your personal value and success against the achievements of friends, foes, family, a celebrity ideal, or a societal model. Remember, you are an original, incapable of being compared to anyone else. Lovingly accept your uniqueness. Don't try to be like someone else, no matter how wonderful you believe that person to be. Your personal challenge is to become more your self, and not a clone of someone else. When you try to copy the qualities of others, you neglect your responsibility to develop those characteristics and abilities that are uniquely your own.

Fall in love with your self by understanding that you are in the world to create a happy, fulfilling life, and not to suffer and struggle. The so-called Christian work ethic that says you are here to sweat and strain is neither Christian nor ethical, and it blocks natural self-love. After all, how can you develop self-love if you believe you're little more than a workhorse?

Fall in love with your self by appreciating your *whole* self, body, mind and soul. You may have been taught to love your soul and hate your body. (The jury is still "out" regarding your mind.) You may have been told that spirit is good but flesh is evil. That is an absurd attitude. Flesh is a physical manifestation of spirit. If flesh is bad, then the spirit must be evil, too.

ALL ABOUT EVIL

Believing themselves to be evil, many people withhold natural self-love. Others believe their fellow man is evil, or the world is evil. But exactly what is the true nature of evil?

Contrary to popular belief, evil is not a cosmic force or devil responsible for sinful, malevolent actions and the woes of the world. Rather than a hellish power, evil is the ignorance of the laws of nature that causes the individual to harm others and poorly create his own life. On a global level, evil is the mass ignorance that causes humankind to violate the natural law, thus creating negative world conditions, such as wars.

For some, believing there is no Devil is more difficult than discovering that there is no Santa Claus. But like Santa, Satan is a fictional character. He was created by ancient religion to objectify the ignorance that separates us from self-knowledge, and the knowledge of our Original Source, or God. Once again, Satan is a fictional, not factual, being—a symbol for *ignorance*. Instead of saying, "The Devil made me do it," you could more accurately state, "Ignorance made me do it."

You may rightly accuse your self of being ignorant, but you are not inherently evil. You are good and worthy of your own love. But you possess free will, and if you choose to *believe* that you are evil, then your behavior will express that belief. In other words, the belief that you are evil will create the physical evidence that you are evil. As always, you create your experiences based upon your beliefs.

But you will not win an eternal heaven, much less create a happy life, by believing that you are evil, or by denying the desires of the flesh. Your personal triumph over ignorance, or "evil," depends upon the knowledge that you gain by working with your *total* self—body, mind and spirit—and not against it.

IS THIS GUILT TRIP REALLY NECESSARY?

Often it is a sense of guilt that keeps you from falling in love with your self. But natural guilt isn't meant to separate you from self-love. Simply put, the purpose of guilt is to remind you to act better in the future. Your inner self points out, "Behaving that way didn't make you feel good, so don't do that again!"

Natural guilt is meant to be a teacher. The lesson is this: To feel better, you need to behave better. After you have changed the guilt-producing action, you are in harmony with the natural law, and the guilt disappears.

Guilt was never meant to imply punishment, either self-inflicted or administered by others. The "marriage" of guilt and punishment is a cultural union, not a natural one. It is only because we *believe* guilt requires punishment that we create situations in which we are punished. Sadly, self-love is frequently sacrificed on the altar of our guilt.

The purpose of natural guilt, to remind you to behave better, has largely been forgotten. Today, humankind manufactures an unnatural guilt that serves no good purpose. It's not a self-generated teaching mechanism, but an artificially induced bad feeling about your self, accepted from others, usually when you don't do what they want you to do.

Here are two examples of natural guilt and unnatural guilt:

Natural Guilt: You feel bad about throwing your father's wheelchair down a flight of stairs—with your father in it!

Unnatural Guilt: You feel bad about not going into the family business because your father wants you in the business, even though you have no interest in it.

Natural Guilt: You feel bad about cheating on your husband because you have promised him sexual fidelity.

Unnatural Guilt: You feel bad about even *looking* at another man, because your husband tells you that it's wrong to find other men attractive.

In both examples, natural guilt can indicate a better way of behaving, the unnatural guilt serves no useful purpose; it just makes you feel bad about your self. Distinguish natural guilt from unnatural guilt in your own life; learn from the former, reject the latter.

LOVE DOES NOT DEMAND SACRIFICE

Sometimes loved ones would have us accept an unnatural guilt when we are unwilling to prove our love by making a personal sacrifice.

The father insists, "If you *really* loved me, you'd come into the family business."

The husband pouts, "If you *really* loved me, you'd never even look at another man."

If you believe that love implies sacrifice, then you will accept a bad feeling about your self whenever you refuse to do the bidding of a loved one. Accepting this unnatural guilt benefits neither you nor the loved one. When you do something for someone out of guilt, rather than desire, they know it, and your sacrifice doesn't really help them.

True love is selfless; it is given to the loved one without wanting sacrifice in payment, or demanding sacrifice to prove that the love is reciprocated. True love is given joyfully, with no expectations, no qualifications and no limitations.

Helping loved ones is important, but doing what is right for you must come first. You are responsible for creating your own happiness; you cannot assume responsibility for the happiness of someone else, no matter how much you love that person.

In reality, the so-called self-sacrificing individual is frequently a person who avoids confronting the challenge of his own life by losing himself in someone else's life. This is not unselfish and virtuous, but a way of dodging self-responsibility.

The "self-sacrificing" father who claims, "I gave up my dreams, and spent thirty years in a thankless job in order to support my family," is really saying, "I didn't believe my dreams were worth much," or, "I didn't believe I was capable of making my dreams come true." This man didn't sacrifice anything; he created the life that he believed he deserved.

Accept self-responsibility, then pursue your life in a joyful, creative, loving manner. Help your self, and you will automatically help your loved ones, and humankind at large.

WORSHIP YOUR SELF

The dictionary defines worship as, "reverent love and allegiance...ardent, humble devotion."

Many of us have been told to worship God, but few of us have been told to worship the god within us. I rarely say that something is impossible, but I'm about to make an exception: It is impossible to worship any god, or truly love anyone, if you don't first love and worship your self. That's because you can only give to others what you possess yourself.

People who claim to worship a god, or love an individual, without first loving and worshipping themselves, are not really honoring the object of their devotion. They are, in effect, "passing the buck"—placing responsibility for their happiness upon the shoulders of the worshipped one. That kind of adoration is something anyone, or any god, can live without.

Discover the god within you and worship your self. Love, honor and cherish your self before making similiar vows to another. By so doing, you will fulfill any responsibility that your Creator, or any person, could reasonably expect you to assume.

ADVENTURE 9

A LOVE LETTER TO MY SELF

For most of you, this will be a unique experience. You are going to write a love letter to your self, acknowledging that you are worthy of self-love, and promising to do your best to change any negative beliefs that have kept you from loving your self, or loving your self more fully.

I will be your guide for this adventure. What follows is my first love letter to my self, written in 1976, after developing the process I then called "Re-Creating My Self."

YOUR GUIDE FOR ADVENTURE 9

CHRISTOPHER, 28 YEARS OLD:

Dear Christopher,

This letter is long overdue. A lot of negative attitudes have kept me from writing it sooner. Now I realize it was unfair of me to judge you on the basis of those ridiculous, false beliefs.

Are you sitting down?

What I'm trying to say is, I love you! I know you never thought you'd hear me say those words, much less write them. But I mean it, I love you, just the way you are.

After examining why I withheld my love for so long, I came to understand that I resented you for not being able to fit in with your family, or your peers. You were never the model son, or one of the gang. You were different, and I didn't like that. I thought you were a misfit, and I believed misfits were unlikable, unlovable—basically worthless.

Today I know that your individuality and your courage in expressing it should have made me love you from the start. You are an original, and I wouldn't have it any other way.

Now, don't get a swelled head. I'm not saying you're Mr. Perfect, but I am saying that you don't need to be Mr. Perfect for me to love you. I can love you for the good person you are right now, and I can look forward to the even better person you will become.

I'm committing myself to loving you even more in the future. I can do this by discarding the other negative attitudes that have kept me from appreciating you more fully. I understand that this represents a lifetime commitment, but I can think of no one who better deserves that kind of devotion.

This is my first love letter to you, but I promise, it won't be my last.

> With sincere affection,
> Christopher

10

AFFIRMING YOUR NEW SELF

"**D**ay by day, in every way, I am getting better and better." That's the world's best known affirmation, created by Emile Coué (1857-1926), a French pharmacist turned psychotherapist, and a champion of self-help.

An affirmation is a positive declaration about your self, stated as fact. Affirmations have long been a staple of self-help books, personal improvement techniques and inspira-tional sermons—especially those based on the positive-thinking philosophy. They are a valuable tool for change. Affirming your *new* self can reverse negative thought pat-terns, thereby helping you accept positive beliefs.

For example, if your thoughts automatically and regu-larly tell you, "My life is becoming worse all the time," then using the affirmation, "Day by day, in every way, I'm getting better and better," can help you break that automatic, negative thinking and introduce a new point of view.

Though affirming your *new* self is an effective tool for personal change, the power of affirmations has been largely misunderstood and exaggerated. All too frequently self-help books suggest that these positive declarations are a virtual cure-all for personal problems, which they aren't. You can better use this tool if you understand what affirm-ing your *new* self can accomplish, as well as what it can't.

FIRST, THE BAD NEWS

Many authors have glorified the power of positive thinking and the benefits of affirmations. This author is going to be different. I'm going to point out their inherent limitations.

Recently, a young woman came to talk to me about *Re-Creating Your Self.* She had read several best-selling books that advocated positive thinking as a panacea for personal problems. Having subsequently practiced what those books preached, she was disappointed with the results. Now she was skeptical of all self-improvement philosophies.

As she put it, "I tried positive thinking for months! I repeated those damn affirmations until I was hoarse, and nothing changed except my *voice.*"

"Did you come to *believe* the ideas your affirmations suggested?" I asked.

"No," she answered, without hesitation.

"In addition to repeating affirmations, what else did you do to help you change your negative attitudes?"

"Nothing much," she replied. "Those books claimed that positive thinking alone would pretty much do the trick."

I explained that positive thinking alone couldn't transform her into the person she wants to be, living the life she desires. "Take two affirmations and call me in the morning" is *not* an effective prescription for happiness. Positive thinking and affirmations are *tools* for change, not a cure-all. Because your beliefs generate the thoughts you have, and not the other way around, the real power is in positive *believing*.

My peeved positive thinker could have repeated her affirmations till she got laryngitis, but if she didn't come to accept the *beliefs* behind her positive thoughts, she would remain unhappy with the results.

In other words, you can't just affirm, "I am good and deserving," and expect your self to accept that positive attitude if you believe, "I'm an unworthy sinner." Without a helping hand from the other tools for change, positive thinking and affirmations will not change long-held negative beliefs.

NOW, THE GOOD NEWS

Once you understand that the real power is in positive believing, then affirmations—used in tandem with the other tools for personal change—can become efficient helpers. Affirming your *new* self means saying "yes" to becoming the person you want to be, living the life you desire.

In Chapter 4, I pointed out that you can begin identifying additional beliefs by paying careful attention to your thoughts, and by listening to the conversations you have with your self throughout the day. These thoughts and inner dialogues support your beliefs and help form your experiences. They strongly influence the way you feel about your self, others and the world.

Affirmations are thought conditioners. Affirming your *new* self can reverse those thoughts that reinforce the negative beliefs you want to discard. For example, if you believe you are an unlovable person, an examination of your thoughts will reveal that they automatically and repeatedly support that negative belief. Introducing and repeating an affirmation such as, "I am naturally lovable and I attract loving people into my life," can help you break the negative-thinking habit and also give you a new attitude about your self to consider. Each time you affirm your *new* self, the negative thought pattern becomes less powerful and automatic.

Affirming your *new* self doesn't mean that you should dislike the person you are right now. On the contrary, an important part of *Re-Creating Your Self* is appreciating your *now* self even as you create your *new* self. Affirming your *new* self isn't meant to be a method for suppressing negative thoughts and feelings. It's important that you experience all of your thoughts and feelings, including the negative ones. Without disliking your self or denying your feelings, affirming your *new* self is a very good way of giving "equal time" to the positive beliefs you want to accept.

HOW TO DO IT

(1) Take five minutes twice a day to affirm your *new* self. Relax, then slowly repeat one affirmation over and over, silently or aloud. The best times to do this are right before you fall asleep at night and immediately upon awakening in the morning.

Your mind is most relaxed at those times and more receptive to thought conditioning.

(2) Affirm your *new* self after experiencing negative thoughts and feelings. Allow your self to fully experience your negative thoughts and feelings; then afterwards, when you're feeling better, use an affirmation to give your *new* self "equal time."

(3) Affirm your *new* self on tape. Record your affirmations on audio tape. Play the tape when you're cleaning house, relaxing in a warm tub, or driving to the store. If you have a video camera and recorder, video tape your self repeating the affirmations, then watch as you affirm your *new* self on television. If you don't have video equipment, try affirming your *new* self while looking in the mirror.

(4) Affirm your *new* self in writing. Select one of your affirmations, then write it out 20 or 30 times in succession. Keep your attention focused on the meaning of the words you write.

(5) Print copies of an affirmation in bold letters. Tape copies to bedroom and bathroom mirrors, your refrigerator, your desk, the dashboard of your car, etc.—wherever it will regularly catch your eye.

(6) Affirm your *new* self during meditation, self-hypnosis and creative daydreaming. (These techniques are explained in Chapters 11 and 12.)

MAKING THE MOST OF YOUR AFFIRMATIONS

(1) At first, use affirmations to recondition negative thoughts related to a belief that you feel will be easy to change. For example, let's say that you are close to discarding the negative belief, "I'm a clumsy person" and almost ready to fully accept the positive belief, "I am poised and well-bal-

anced." This would be a good first belief for you to affirm, because it's one that you have already partially accepted. After you've gained experience, use affirmations related to your more difficult challenges.

(2) Suspend disbelief while affirming your *new* self. While you're in the process of accepting a new belief, you may find your self affirming, "I deserve the best of everything," while still partially believing, "I'm unworthy of my heart's desires." Try your best to temporarily suspend disbelief while affirming your *new* self. Play-act for a while. Pretend that you believe you deserve the best of everything. Repeat your affirmation in a sincere voice and try to *feel* deserving.

(3) Affirm your *new* self with statements that feel right for you. Don't use affirmations that contain words and phrases that feel awkward or uncomfortable.

(4) Continue to use an affirmation until you achieve your goal—or until you change your goal.

AFFIRMATIONS YOU CAN USE

You can start affirming your *new* self right now with the following positive declarations. Use the affirmations that apply to your goals. If the words feel right, repeat the affirmation verbatim. If they don't, change them to suit your personal needs.

HEALTH

- I am the radiant picture of health—physically, mentally and spiritually.
- Day by day, in every way, I am becoming healthier and stronger.
- I am glowingly healthy and radiate dynamic energy.

- Healing energy now streams through every cell in my body. I give thanks for my good health.

HAPPINESS
- Happiness is my birthright. I claim it *now*!
- My happiness is my affair; therefore, no one can interfere.
- I'm ready right now to accept all the happiness life has to offer.
- My heart's desires now flow to me in a steady, unbroken, ever-increasing stream of happiness.

SELF-LOVE
- I am naturally lovable, both to myself and to others.
- The more I love myself, the more I can love others.
- I love myself *now*, just as I am.
- I am naturally good, trustworthy and valuable.

RE-CREATING YOUR SELF
- I now accept the power and the privilege to become the person I want to be, living the life I desire.
- Personal change is not just possible—it's unstoppable!
- I alone control my destiny. The power to make the changes I desire is mine.
- Change is the natural order, so naturally I'm ordering change.

RELATIONSHIPS
- Day by day, in every way, my relationship with _____ is getting better and better.
- I am naturally lovable, so naturally I attract loving relationships.
- I am now ready to accept a happy, loving, lasting relationship.
- The relationship I'm seeking is now seeking me!

CAREER

- The career success I desire is now coming to me, effortlessly and in a perfect way.
- I have a wonderful career with wonderful pay. I provide a wonderful service in a wonderful way.
- Loving myself, I now attract lucrative, fulfilling career opportunities into my life.
- I love my job and I am richly rewarded, financially and creatively.

GENERAL WELL-BEING

- I am a magnet for health, happiness, prosperity and love.
- I deserve the best of everything, so I create the very best.
- My beliefs create my reality, and I believe I deserve success in all areas of my life.
- Right now I possess within me everything I need to create the life I desire.

ADVENTURE 10

AFFIRMING MY <u>NEW</u> SELF

STEP 1: Open your logbook to Adventure 7, your blueprint for personal change.

STEP 2: One at a time, review the new beliefs you want to accept.

STEP 3: On a blank page in your logbook, copy your new beliefs, leaving enough room after each one to write an affirmation.

STEP 4: Using the guidelines on the next page, create your own affirmation for each of your new beliefs.

STEP 5: Put your self-created affirmations to work.

CREATING EFFECTIVE AFFIRMATIONS

(1) The best affirmations are short and sweet, no longer than two brief sentences.

(2) Phrase your affirmations in the most positive way. For example, don't say, "I'm clumsy, but I can change." Declare, "I am poised, centered and in perfect balance."

(3) Affirm your *new* self in the present tense, as if the new you already exists. Don't write, "I will learn to love myself." Affirm, "I love myself *now*, just the way I am."

(4) Remember to use words and phrasing that feel right to you.

YOUR GUIDE FOR ADVENTURE 10

Lee, your guide for Adventure 7, will provide a format you can use for this adventure.

RELATIONSHIPS

New belief: *When I'm ready, I can have a relationship, or even a second marriage, that will be happy and meaningful.*

Affirming my new self: *My desire for happiness now attracts happy, meaningful relationships into my life.*

AGING

New belief: *My ability to make successful changes doesn't decrease with age, and that includes my ability to change careers.*

Affirming my new self: *Like wine, I get better with age. I'm now better able to make the changes I desire.*

CAREER

New belief: *My career can become exciting and challenging again. There is always something new to learn about any business.*

Affirming my new self: *My endless curiosity creates endless opportunities for me to make my work endlessly fresh and exciting.*

11

RELAX AND RE-CREATE YOUR SELF

*R*e-*Creating Your Self* can be as easy as relaxing. Deep relaxation is the key for effectively using two natural tools for personal change: meditation and self-hypnosis. Both of these simple techniques are highly effective ways to acquire new, positive beliefs and discard old, negative ones. Let me explain how:

Your beliefs shape your life, and those beliefs are expressed through both mental actions and physical actions. But the mental action always exists *first*; the physical action follows, having been initiated by the mental act. Meditation and self-hypnosis are dynamic methods for altering the mental actions that eventually result in your physical experiences.

Everyone is familiar with physical action, but exactly what is a mental action—the inner catalyst that makes the physical action possible? A mental action is an individualized portion of thought-energy generated and shaped by a belief. A mental action is always based upon your ideas about reality. It represents your inner readiness and agreement to allow a specific physical action to occur. Once created, the mental action works to transform the inner information into a physical experience.

Both meditation and self-hypnosis allow you to introduce and encourage positive mental actions that will eventually create the physical experiences you desire. Relaxation is the fundamental and indispensable basis for effectively using these two potent tools for change.

Meditation and self-hypnosis have many other things in common besides relaxation. Consider these important similarities:

- Both are completely natural methods of self-improvement.
- Both methods are active, not passive. The individual initiates specific mental actions.
- Both are dependent on the individual's self-direction and determination.
- Both methods require concentration.
- Both strive to decrease the individual's field of attention and increase the intensity of attention.
- Both methods speak to the inner self.
- Both influence major areas of behavior.

- Both methods can benefit almost anyone in a short period of time.
- Both meditation and self-hypnosis are largely misunderstood by the public—shrouded in mystery and misconceptions. The so-called experts have made these simple, natural tools for change appear complicated and inaccessible.

I'm going to demystify and simplify meditation and self-hypnosis for you, and give you easy guidelines for using these methods to re-create your self.

BASIC MEDITATION

Basic meditation is really very simple. But many people have been led to believe that it is a difficult, rigid discipline, a state of physical detachment far beyond the abilities of most mortals. By and large, meditation is perceived to be the domain of spiritual masters who already have one bare foot on a higher plane. These false beliefs are misleading and intimidating. In truth, basic meditation is accessible to anyone who wants to use it.

Quite simply, meditation is the process of directing the conscious mind inward in order to concentrate upon and examine a single subject. The meditator's increased concentration on his subject automatically filters out conscious awareness of other stimuli.

In everyday life, your mind automatically filters the stimuli you perceive. This filtering mechanism is a protective device that prevents your central nervous system from becoming overstimulated and "blowing a fuse." In meditation, you consciously use your mind's natural ability to focus attention and filter stimuli. Your attention is focused on the subject of your meditation and you filter out stimuli unrelated to your subject.

To meditate successfully, you don't need anything that you don't already have. You don't need a teacher. You don't need spiritual faith. You don't need to become "one with the universe." Becoming one with the subject of your meditation is good enough. You don't need to buy a mantra from a guru, burn incense, chant, or twist your body into a lotus position.

What you do need to meditate successfully is basic. You need a *subject* for meditation. You need the *desire* to meditate. You need the *willpower* to do it regularly. (Even 15 minutes a day can produce surprisingly successful results.)

HOW TO DO IT

Actually, you already know how to meditate. You do it frequently, naturally and automatically. When you're stopped in traffic, your mind on a business meeting, only peripherally aware of the cars and noise around you, you are meditating. When you're in front of the bathroom mirror, shaving automatically, mentally rehashing an argument you've had with a friend, you're meditating. And you're meditating at the laundromat when you watch your clothes spin in the dryer but think about the date you had the night before. In other words, whenever you shut out extraneous stimuli and focus your attention on a single subject, you're meditating.

Right now, you can start using meditation as a practical and efficient tool for change by following these simple guidelines:

(1) Choose the subject of your meditation. If meditation is for the purpose of *Re-Creating Your Self*, then your subject might be a new belief you want to accept.

(2) Select a quiet, pleasant place for your meditation. That place can be indoors or outdoors—your bedroom, a quiet park or beach.

(3) Assume a comfortable position, whatever that means to you. You can even lie down. I often do.

(4) Close your eyes and relax. Use your own technique for natural relaxation, or use the relaxation exercise printed near the end of this chapter.

(5) Focus your attention on the subject of your meditation. To the best of your ability disregard stimuli, both external and internal, unrelated to your subject. If your mind wanders, be patient with your self. If you have thoughts unrelated to your meditation, acknowledge them, then return to your subject. Your ability to concentrate will increase with practice.

(6) Examine and evaluate all aspects of your subject. If your subject is a new belief, analyze it from all angles. Ask your self questions. How have you limited your self by not accepting the belief? How will accepting the belief improve the quality of your life? What is keeping you from accepting the belief right now?

(7) Finish your meditation slowly and peacefully. When you're ready to end your session, open your eyes. Give your self a few moments to return your attention to its usual focus. Try to carry the relaxation of your meditation into the rest of the day.

It's important to remember that the best way to meditate is the way that works best for you. So if you have any ideas for improving the quality of your meditation, give them a try. Again, meditation is a creative process, not a harsh discipline.

NATURAL HYPNOSIS

People have at least as many misconceptions about hypnosis as they do about meditation. We can thank the entertainment industry for that. As fictitiously practiced on TV and in the movies, hypnosis is hocus-pocus that robs its subject of free will. The subject is most usually depicted as a zombie-like victim under the power of a hypnotist. The hypnotist is commonly a wild-eyed psychopath who commands the subject to commit dastardly crimes, including murder. This hokey scenario has been the source of many bad films and TV shows. Even worse, it has perpetuated damaging myths and misconceptions about hypnosis.

Nightclub entertainers haven't helped, either. Many stage hypnotists are performers first and hypnotists second. These unrepentant hams typically glide onstage singing "On A Clear Day You Can See Forever," then "command" hypnotized audience members to do foolish things, such as stripping down to their skivvies or barking like a dog. Surprisingly, some people even obey these silly performers, though not because they're under the power of a hammy hypnotist. Most often these people enjoy their momentary celebrity and willingly go along with the stage performance.

Because hypnosis is so widely misunderstood and maligned, many people who could benefit by using this important tool for change have been scared away. Don't be one of those people.

In fact, if not in fiction, hypnosis is simply a natural state of deep relaxation in which you concentrate upon a specific area of thought and introduce suggestions concerning that area of thought.

Many people believe that a hypnotized person is asleep or unconscious, but neither is true. This misunderstanding is the result of early techniques for inducing hypnosis that included such misleading wording as, "You are getting *sleepy*," and "All the muscles of your body are going to *sleep.*" Today, hypnotists more accurately induce hypnosis with phrases such as, "You are becoming more and more *relaxed,*" and, "All the muscles of your body are becoming more deeply *relaxed.*"

Hypnosis depends upon the subject's ability to focus attention on a chosen area of thought. Therefore, it is absolutely necessary for a hypnotized person to be *awake and conscious* at all times, even in the deepest stages of hypnosis. A hypnotized person is never asleep or unconscious, because a person can't concentrate on anything in those states.

Some people are afraid that they won't "wake up" after being hypnotized. But once it's understood that the subject isn't asleep at all—just deeply relaxed—this fear becomes groundless. A hypnotized person can end hypnosis at will and return his attention to its usual focus.

Another false belief is that a hypnotized person is under the control of the hypnotist and must do his bidding, whatever the suggestion. Nothing could be further from the truth. The subject is never "under the power" of the hypnotist, nor will he carry out suggestions that are against his principles, or otherwise unacceptable. Just ask one of the thousands of people who have failed to quit smoking through hypnosis. Intellectually these smokers may have felt that they *should* quit. But they really *didn't want to* quit. Consequently, hypnotic suggestions to quit were powerless and went unheeded. Under hypnosis, you will only act upon those suggestions that you consciously want to accept.

NATURAL SELF-HYPNOSIS

In self-hypnosis you simultaneously act as hypnotist and subject.

When I suggest that a student use this potent tool, I

often hear: "Gee, I don't think I can be hypnotized," or "I don't think I could ever learn to hypnotize myself." In either case, I answer confidently, "You can if you want to." That's because virtually anyone can learn to relax and concentrate and, basically, that's all there is to self-hypnosis.

Like meditation, self-hypnosis is something you already do naturally and spontaneously. For example, you have literally hypnotized your self into accepting your current beliefs: You focused your attention upon them and filtered out contradictory stimuli. Then you accepted suggestions regarding those beliefs and acted upon them.

Whenever you focus upon a specific area of thought, with your attention basically unaffected by stimuli unrelated to that area of thought, you're hypnotizing your self. You are frequently in a self-induced hypnotic state while reading a book, watching a concert, movie or TV show, or making love.

You give your self hypnotic suggestions almost constantly. Once again, examine your thoughts and inner commentaries. They are powerful auto-suggestions, based upon your attitudes about life, a personal focus that largely ignores stimuli unrelated to your particular belief system.

HOW TO DO IT

By following these simple guidelines you can start using natural self-hypnosis today to introduce and encourage your new beliefs:

(1) Select your topic for self-hypnosis.
(2) Create one specific suggestion for your session. A hypnotic suggestion is a positive statement about your self that is related to the topic of your session. For example, if your topic is the new belief, "I am

a good person, worthy of the best life has to offer," then your suggestion for that session might be, "With each passing day, I will become more and more aware of my personal goodness and value."

Like an affirmation, a hypnotic suggestion should be short and worded in the most positive manner. Phrase your suggestion in a way that describes a process of *becoming* rather than as a change already achieved. This allows time for the suggestion to be accepted and carried out. For example, if you are ill, don't suggest, "I am perfectly healthy right now." Instead suggest, "I am becoming healthier all the time."

(3) Memorize your suggestion.

(4) Select a quiet, pleasant place for your session.

(5) Assume a comfortable position.

(6) Close your eyes and relax. The relaxation exercise described later in the chapter is especially good for hypnosis.

(7) Make your self even more deeply relaxed. Aloud or mentally, tell your self, "With every passing moment, I am becoming more and more deeply relaxed." Repeat this slowly, four or five times.

(8) Focus your attention upon the topic of your session. Think about the satisfaction you'll feel when you achieve your goal.

(9) Slowly repeat your suggestion over and over, either mentally or aloud, whichever you prefer. Don't repeat the suggestion mechanically but concentrate on what you are saying. Feel the meaning behind the suggestion. Five to ten minutes of this repetition is enough.

(10) When you're ready to end the session, just think or say, "I am now ready to end my self-hypnosis." Suggest to your self, "When I open my eyes, I will feel completely refreshed, wonderful and filled

with relaxed energy." Then count slowly from one to five.

(11) Open your eyes. Give your self a few moments to adjust to your usual focus.

Assisted by the guidelines in this chapter, you can put meditation and self-hypnosis to work for you right away. Students sometimes ask, "What's the basic difference between the two techniques?" It is this: In meditation you focus your attention upon a single subject, then you examine your subject as creatively and completely as possible. In self-hypnosis, you focus your attention upon a specific area of thought, then you introduce positive suggestions pertaining to that area of thought. After trying both methods, many people find they have a preference for one or the other. If this proves to be true for you, use the method you enjoy most.

You will use either method more effectively by: (1) practicing daily, if possible, at the same time and place, (2) being patient with your self and non-critical of your progress, (3) working to improve your concentration in all areas of your life, and (4) developing a greater respect for the value of self-analysis.

RELAXING YOUR SELF

Every aspect of your life is enhanced when you're relaxed. Adopt an easy-does-it attitude. Try to do everything a little more slowly, peacefully and assuredly.

When you're relaxed, your brain-wave pattern changes from its usual beta level to a slower level, called alpha. This slower alpha level is necessary for meditation and self-hypnosis.

You can use the following relaxation exercise to achieve alpha before beginning meditation or self-hypnosis. Put this exercise on tape. Read the words slowly and clearly in a monotone voice.

Assume a comfortable position in a quiet, pleasant place, then close your eyes and begin.

"My whole body is becoming limp and relaxed.

"The muscles in my scalp and forehead are becoming very comfortable and relaxed ... My eyebrows relax ... The area all around my eyes relaxes ... Now the tiny muscles of my eyelids relax, and the relaxation flows deep inside my mouth, and all the muscles in my mouth relax.

"The relaxation spreads deep into the back of my throat ... deep in back of my head and neck ... deep into my neck and shoulders.

"Now my arms relax ... my upper arms relax ... As I concentrate on my forearms, I feel them relax ... All the muscles between my elbows and my wrists relax ... I feel the relaxation spreading across the tops of my hands and deep into my hands ... deep through my hands to the palms ... Now my fingers relax ... all the way to the finger tips.

"Returning my attention to the relaxed muscles of my neck and shoulders, I let the relaxation flow into my chest and lungs. My breathing becomes easy and gentle. I feel myself becoming more deeply relaxed with each gentle and easy breath. All outside sounds are unimportant now. I do not allow any outside sounds to disturb my deep relaxation.

"Now the relaxation spreads deep into the broad of my back. I feel it flow gently down my back to the small of my back. All the muscles of my body are becoming more and more relaxed, but I remain perfectly conscious, aware and focused.

"The relaxation spreads around and deep into my sides. All the muscles of my abdomen relax ... deep into my abdomen ... All the muscles of my abdomen and hips relax.

"Now my legs relax. I feel the relaxation flowing into my thighs and knees ... My calves relax—all the way to my ankles ... My feet relax ... The heels of my feet relax ... The undersides of my feet—deep through my feet to the tops ... And, finally, even my toes relax ... It feels so good to let go of all tension and care and be completely relaxed."

ADVENTURE 11

RELAXING INTO MY <u>NEW</u> SELF

STEP 1: Using the guidelines for basic meditation in this chapter, meditate upon one of your new beliefs.

STEP 2: The next day, make the subject of your previous day's meditation the topic of a session in self-hypnosis. Use the guidelines for natural self-hypnosis in this chapter.

STEP 3: After you've tried both of these methods, compare the two. Ask your self these questions and write the answers in your logbook. Which did you like best? Why? Did you find both methods equally enjoyable? Which do you feel will most effectively help you make the changes you desire?

Use meditation or self-hypnosis on a daily basis to help you accomplish your goals. If you like both methods equally well, and you have the time, there's no reason not to use both.

12

IMAGINE YOUR NEW SELF

Imagination is the mental formation of an image or concept that is not physically real or present. But imagination isn't just fantasy. Whatever you imagine is created mentally and is real on that level. Imagination is mental reality.

Imagination is one of humankind's most purely creative processes. Undirected, it is also one of the most fickle. Sometimes we imagine that which we fear and don't want to see physically created—an illness, an accident, poverty, war. Other times we imagine that which we strongly desire—health, success, money, a new lover or a new car. This chapter is about training your self to consciously use your imagination in a way that will help you accept your new beliefs.

CREATIVE DAYDREAMING

Like positive thinking, imagination has been a cornerstone of many self-improvement methods. It has variously been called creative visualization, dynamic imaging, positive picturizing and mental imagery.

In *Re-Creating Your Self*, imagination as a tool for personal change is called creative daydreaming. I like that term because everyone knows what daydreaming is, and how to do it. In fact, many students tell me that they remember daydreams more vividly than physical experiences.

For most of us, daydreaming begins very early in life. During childhood, daydreams rescue you from boring school lessons or church services and place you in a more exciting environment. Though you physically remain in arithmetic class, mentally you slay a fire-breathing dragon, hit a home run, or skinny dip with your heartthrob in a blue lagoon.

In adulthood, you make similar use of daydreams to escape the doldrums of a dull job, or the stupefying boredom of some meeting, lecture or ceremony that you feel compelled to attend. And let's not forget sexual fantasies. They are frequently the subject of our most intense daydreams.

One of the reasons creative daydreaming is such a trusty tool for personal change is that most of us are already experts in this area.

A dictionary definition of *daydream* is "a mental fantasy while awake that fulfills wishes, hopes or desires." Your creative daydreams are going to utilize your imagination to *fulfill* your *wish* to become the person you want to be, living the life you *desire*.

There are a few basic differences between your usual daydreams and the creative daydreams involved in *Re-Creating Your Self*:

- Creative daydreaming is a planned event. Your usual daydreams are spontaneous.
- In creative daydreaming you choose your theme in advance. The theme of your usual daydream is most often chosen at random.
- The theme of a creative daydream is something that is obtainable in physical life, such as a better paying job, a loving relationship, a trimmer body. In a regular daydream, your theme may not be obtainable. For example, where but in your imagination will you find a fire-breathing dragon to slay?

WHY CREATIVE DAYDREAMING WORKS

Your beliefs, expressed through mental and physical actions, create your life. The mental action always exists first and determines the kind of physical action that will later occur.

Because imagination produces mighty mental actions, we tend to eventually create physically that which we imagine. For better or worse, the more intensely we imagine something, the more likely it is to be manifested physically. That's why it's so important to train our imagination to create positive mental actions.

Regrettably, many people most strongly imagine failure, illness, loneliness and other unhappy conditions, so that's what they create physically. However, we can train ourselves to vividly imagine success, health and happiness;

by doing so, we help create our *new* self in fact. That's what creative daydreaming is all about.

Creative daydreams propel your affirmations a dynamic step further. When you imagine your *new* self, you do more than declare your *new* self with words, you mentally *see* your *new* self as if it already exists. In fact, your *new* self is a mental reality as soon as you create it in your imagination. Once your *new* self becomes a mental reality, the shape is formed for its physical manifestation.

HOW TO DO IT

Because you use your imagination constantly and in many different ways, imagining your *new* self is, perhaps, the easiest tool to use for personal change. Here are the guidelines for successful creative daydreaming:

(1) Choose the theme of your creative daydream. For *Re-Creating Your Self*, the theme would most likely be one of your new beliefs. When first using this method, select a belief that you feel will be relatively easy for you to accept, or even one you have already partially accepted. Save your more challenging new beliefs for later when you have gained experience with this technique.

(2) Select a quiet, pleasant place to do your creative daydreaming.

(3) Assume a comfortable position.

(4) Close your eyes and relax your self.

(5) Affirm the theme of your creative daydream, either mentally or aloud. For example, if your theme is, "I can become slimmer and more attractive," then affirm, "I am now slender, and more attractive than I have ever been in my life."

(6) Mentally create your daydream. Imagine your *new* self as if that self already exists. In a way, it does. The moment you imagine your *new* self, that self becomes a mental reality.

Create your daydream vividly and include as many details as possible. Using the same example, you would visualize your body as being slender and strong, well-dressed and impeccably groomed. In other words, if becoming slim and more attractive is your goal, then you must imagine this even more intensely than in fear you imagine becoming unattractive. Remember, the intensity of *any* mental action, including a creative daydream, largely determines how quickly it will be created as a physical reality.

(7) Bring your other senses into your daydream. In the "slim and attractive" daydream, you might slowly run a hand over your *new* self, mentally "feeling" your slender, strong body. "Feel" the positive emotions generated by looking so attractive. "Smell" and "taste" the healthy foods that keep your *new* self in great shape. "Hear" your friends say, "You've never looked better in your life!"

(8) Try to sustain your creative daydream for ten to fifteen minutes. Mentally create different scenes and situations related to your theme. But don't strain your self. Creative daydreaming is meant to be a fun, playful process. At first, you may find it difficult to sustain your daydream for more than a few minutes. That's all right. Your ability to imagine your *new* self will automatically increase with practice.

(9) End your creative daydream with the same affirmation you used to begin it. Slowly repeat the affirmation four or five times, then open your eyes.

MAKING THE MOST OF YOUR CREATIVE DAYDREAMS

Practice creative daydreaming daily. As is the case with affirmations, creative daydreaming is especially effective when practiced just before you fall asleep at night or immediately after awakening in the morning.

As you do when affirming your *new* self, try to suspend disbelief during your creative daydreams. Become a daydream believer. For the length of your session, believe that your goal has already been attained. If suspending disbelief becomes impossible, and contradictory thoughts arise, don't struggle to suppress them. Trying too hard to prevent negative thoughts most often increases their hold on you. Instead, allow these thoughts to move through your mind, then return to the positive theme of your daydream.

Don't become upset if ideas unrelated to your theme interrupt your daydream. Acknowledge those stray ideas, then gently return your attention to your theme.

Be patient. Don't expect the mental reality of your creative daydream to manifest itself as a physical reality overnight (although it occasionally happens almost that fast). Repeat the same daydream theme until your goal is accomplished, or until you change your goal.

Use creative daydreaming in tandem with meditation and self-hypnosis. In meditation, bring visualization into the examination and evaluation of your subject. In hypnosis, after you've finished repeating your suggestion, mentally see what you've suggested as being real in your life.

ADVENTURE 12

IMAGINING MY <u>NEW</u> SELF

STEP 1: Return to Adventure 7, your blueprint for personal change. Review your new beliefs, then select one that you feel will be relatively easy to accept, or even one that you have already partially accepted.

STEP 2: Following the guidelines in this chapter, make the belief you selected the theme of a creative daydream.

13

RE-CREATING YOUR SELF IN YOUR *SLEEP*

In my quest to discover *all* the tools available for re-creating my self, I was led—though reluctantly—to re-examine my beliefs about the value of dreams. I was reluctant, because I was raised to believe that dreams are basically meaningless, uncontrollable experiences without any practical usefulness to waking life and the "real" world.

Fortunately for me, friends whom I respect believed dreams to be an important tool for personal change and self-understanding and, eventually, they persuaded me to re-evaluate my attitude.

My subsequent studies and experiments proved that my old beliefs about dreams were false and limiting. My friends had been right. I discovered first-hand that dream experiences are meaningful, therapeutic and beneficial to everyday life. Furthermore, I learned that I could train my self to better remember dreams and to create specific dreams that I wanted to have. But I'm getting ahead of my self.

THE IMPORTANCE OF DREAMS

For 25 years I had accepted the prevailing cultural belief that dreams are basically inconsequential, so I hadn't considered something that now seems obvious:

Dreams are powerful, highly creative mental actions. Because our beliefs, expressed through physical and *mental* actions, create our reality, dreams are important to our life.

The more I examined my own dreams, the more I wondered why I—and humankind at large—had foolishly ignored the importance of dreams, a nightly mental activity. (On the average, people spend about one and a half hours each night dreaming.) Later, reading books about dreams, I learned that we hadn't always overlooked their significance.

In earlier times, people understood that as their waking experiences had meaning and value, so did their dream experiences. The people of many early civilizations, including ancient Egypt, believed that they perceived future events—even created them—in the dream state. Certainly the intimate relationship between the dreamer and his waking self was repeatedly chronicled in both

Testaments of the Bible. (Imagine trying to convince the Biblical Jacob, Joseph and Pharaoh that dreams are meaningless concoctions with no bearing on reality.)

If untold generations had acknowledged the importance of dream experiences, then how had we come to generally disregard them? My theory is this: Humankind, desiring to better understand the physical world and prevail in it, began to discount the value of dreams—along with all other stimuli that weren't perceived by the five physical senses. Humanity's passion for things physical increased through the ages, and eventually, we came to believe that dreams were totally unimportant to "real" life and, therefore, unworthy of serious examination.

These days, most people consider "real life" to be synonymous with "physical life." Mental creations, including dreams, are usually believed to be fantasies. How often has someone disputed the validity of your own personal experience with the phrase, "It's all in your head!" That's just another way of saying, if it's physical, it's real; if it's mental, it's not.

In other times, dream creations were believed to be no less valid than physical constructions. Humankind acknowledged both physical events and dream experiences as real, while understanding the obvious differences between the two levels of reality.

Today we are *slowly* developing a renewed interest and respect for the metaphysical world, including the world of dreams. Actually, dream experiences began regaining a modicum of their former respectability with the advent of modern psychology. Freud spearheaded a minor dream renaissance within the scientific community with his *Interpretation of Dreams* (1900). In that book, Freud stated that dreams were important keys to the makeup of the individual, worthy of careful and extensive study. He also believed that dreams protect sleep by draining off the force of emotional disturbances that would otherwise cause a person to awaken.

Jung, the founder of analytical psychology, went Freud one better. He speculated that we actually try out experiences mentally in dreams before creating those experiences physically in waking life. Jung's theory is similar to the ancient Egyptian belief that physical events are often first created in the dream state. If this is true, then we have an explanation for the occurrence of precognitive dreams—a phenomenon whose documented history spans the recorded history of humankind itself.

My personal experience agrees with that of the Egyptians and Dr. Jung. My dreams, faithfully recorded in a dream diary, sometimes prove to be precognitive, revealing "previews of coming attractions" from everyday life. And I've come to understand "deja vu"—the feeling of having already experienced something that would seem to be a first-time event. When I have the "deja-vu" feeling, I often remember that I have previously dreamed about the physical event I am experiencing.

RE-CREATING YOUR SELF IN YOUR SLEEP—AUTOMATICALLY

How many times have you heard someone say, "I could do that in my sleep!" The implication is that something could be done successfully and effortlessly. You can legitimately say that about *Re-Creating Your Self*: Whether or not you remember your dreams, you automatically re-create your self—both physically and mentally—in your sleep every night.

The sleeping state automatically regenerates your physical body. When your body is asleep, everything slows down. Your rate of metabolism is at its lowest. Your blood pressure drops. Your pulse rate is slower, and so is your breathing. Even your temperature drops slightly. In this restful mode, your body's tired organs and tissues are restored; your blood is cleansed of impurities; repair work is done.

Likewise, the dreams you form while asleep automatically renew you mentally. They give you undisturbed time to work out problems you've been unable to solve while awake. This is one of the most practical and important functions of the dream state—a function that is necessary in order to maintain your personal well-being. In fact, scientific studies reveal that people cannot go for more than a few days without dreaming before they show signs of severe mental stress.

Have you noticed that you need more sleep when you're going through a personal crisis? If you think this extra sleep is just a way of escaping your difficulties, you're wrong. Rather than escaping your problems, you use this time to work them out naturally and automatically on another level—the dream level. When you're faced with a problem, or when you want to change your life, your dreams automatically pitch in and help. In such dreams you experiment with different methods of solving your problem, and you mentally experience the results that each method will produce.

Though you may not consciously remember these therapeutic dreams, your subconscious never forgets. Later, in the waking state, the answer to your problem may seem to come "out of the blue." More likely, you are recalling the solution that yielded the best results in your dream experiments.

In addition to the automatic, therapeutic benefits of dreams, you can consciously use the dream state to help you re-create your self. If you're willing to put in the time and effort, you can create specific dreams, and you can dramatically improve your ability to remember dreams.

REMEMBERING YOUR DREAMS

Some people claim that they don't dream, but this isn't true. Though people differ in their ability to remember dreams, everyone does dream. However, we normally forget more dreams than we remember; even the dreams we recall are usually remembered only in part. This isn't because our ability to recall dreams is inherently limited. Basically, we forget dreams because we don't believe they're worth remembering.

In all areas of life, you tend to consciously remember only those experiences you believe to be significant. For as long as you believe dreams to be inconsequential, you will forget them even as you forget the mundane details of waking life. If you want to better remember your dreams, you must first acknowledge their importance. Then you can use the following simple technique for increasing dream recall:

(1) Get a college ruled notebook—the same kind you're using for your "Adventures in Inner Space"—and make it your dream diary. Keep it, along with a pen or pencil, beside your bed.

(2) Before falling asleep at night, take a few minutes to repeat this affirmation: "Upon awakening tomorrow, I will consciously remember the dreams I have tonight," If you prefer self-hypnosis, suggest, "Each morning will bring a more complete and vivid recall of the dreams I've had the night before."

(3) *Immediately* upon awakening in the morning—before brushing your teeth or making coffee—open your dream diary. Write down the dreams you remember and date them. Leave a generous amount of space after each dream for any additional details you remember later in the day. (If

you awaken during the night with a dream on your mind, don't wait until morning to write it down. Do it immediately.)

Whatever your present level of dream recall, you can increase it by faithfully using this technique. Your remembered dreams may answer simple questions, or yield information about major life challenges. They may help you accept a new belief, or reveal negative attitudes that have previously escaped identification.

Don't be discouraged if it takes a while to increase dream recall to your satisfaction. After years of attaching little or no value to dreams, your conscious mind may need time to fully accept the belief that they are worth remembering. Be patient and persevere.

CREATING SPECIFIC DREAMS

After increasing dream recall, you may want to learn how to create specific dreams. Like waking experiences, dream experiences are of your own creation. They don't just happen to you; you make them happen. They are the constructions of your subconscious mind, and you can direct your subconscious to create specific dreams you want to have. You can ask about any aspect of your life and create a dream that explores the question and provides an answer. This means that you can examine and evaluate beliefs in your sleep. You can create dreams that reveal the barriers preventing you from becoming the person you want to be, living the life you desire.

The method for learning to effectively create specific dreams is similar to the technique for increasing dream recall:

(1) Decide on the subject for one specific dream you

want to have. For *Re-Creating Your Self*, the subject is commonly belief-related. You can request a dream that gives you new insight into a negative belief you want to discard or a positive belief you want to accept. You can ask for a dream that reveals personal attitudes that are keeping you from more quickly discarding or accepting a specific belief.

(2) Before falling asleep, take a few minutes to affirm, "Tonight I will create a dream that gives me new and useful information about (your subject), and I will remember that dream upon awakening." If you prefer self-hypnosis, this same affirmation can also be used as an effective auto-suggestion.

(3) *Immediately* upon awakening, write the dream in your diary. If you don't remember having the dream you requested, then repeat your request each night until you get it, or until the sought-after information comes to you in another way. If the information seems to come "out of the blue," it could mean that you did create the specific dream you asked for, but you didn't consciously remember it. If you request the same dream every night for a week without success, and the desired information doesn't reach you in another way, then relax and ask your self if there is any reason why you might be blocking the information from your conscious awareness.

Keep in mind that your personal beliefs about dreams not only determine your ability to remember them, they also affect your success in creating the specific dreams you ask for. If you desire a certain dream on the one hand, but on the other hand, you don't really believe you can create it, then you automatically undermine your own efforts. As always, your experience will be created in line with your beliefs and expectations, not your desires.

Training the subconscious to create specific dreams isn't for everyone and it's certainly not a prerequisite for successfully *Re-Creating Your Self*—because this particular dream skill takes time and effort to develop. It's not unusual to practice this technique for several months before having any kind of success. But if you have a desire to work more closely with your dreams, and you have the discipline to do it, eventually you will be richly rewarded.

I HEAL MY SELF IN MY SLEEP

This story from my own life is a good example of how creating a specific dream can pay off.

At 25, I was a physically strong and healthy man with endless energy. But within a few short months, all of that changed. I became chronically weak and ill, drained of all power. Hoping that the condition would reverse itself, I put off going to the doctor. But when I became too weak to get out of bed in the morning, I finally gave in and went for a physical examination.

A test for glucose tolerance revealed that I had hypo-glycemia—low blood sugar. After I eliminated sugar from my diet, my strength and health returned. But whenever I "fudged" and ate my beloved chocolate, or anything with sugar, I would promptly feel enervated and ill. Sometimes it seemed that even *smelling* sugar caused me to swoon.

Knowing that I create my experiences—*all* of them—I took responsibility for creating my blood-sugar problem. I also knew that I could re-create it by identifying, then changing, the sour beliefs that had created the illness. But because my new diet eliminated the symptoms, and other areas of my life more urgently needed re-creating, I didn't really try to heal my self.

Ten years later, I was still denying my sweet tooth its

just desserts. Watching me walk away from pastries I obviously coveted, friends would chide, "So Christopher, when are *you* going to become the person you want to be, eating the desserts you desire?" I got their message. It was high time I acted on my own good advice.

I decided to use my dream skills to help cure me of hypoglycemia. Using the procedure described earlier, I requested a dream that would reveal the principal belief that had created the disease. I didn't get my requested dream on the first try, nor on the second or third. Then on the fourth night...

As the dream began, I was a baby, sitting in a highchair in the kitchen of my family's Bronx apartment. Also in the kitchen were my mother and a friend. They were talking about my grandmothers, both of whom had blood-sugar problems. (In real life, both died from diabetes-related causes.) My mother was explaining, "These blood-sugar diseases are hereditary, you know—but they usually *skip a generation*." Hearing this, I reasoned that mommy and daddy were safe, but I was fair game for this kind of illness. I began to cry.

Tears blurred my vision. Then, suddenly, my dream location changed. I was standing in my maternal grand-mother's kitchen. I was a few years older. Both my grand-mothers were huddled around the stove, stirring a big pot of spaghetti sauce. My Aunt Ida entered the room, carrying the biggest chocolate chip cookie I've ever seen—in or out of a dream. She smiled and handed it to me. "It's a shame your grandmothers can't eat sweets," she said sadly. Then she added, "Blood sugar diseases are hereditary, you know—but they usually *skip a generation*." I dropped the cookie. It hit the floor and shattered as if it were glass.

I awakened suddenly, half-expecting to see cookie crumbs on the bed sheets. I scribbled the dream in my diary. Later, reading the entry, I remembered how many times during my childhood I had heard people say, "Blood sugar diseases are hereditary—but they usually *skip a generation*." Although I had long forgotten having heard this belief, I had obviously accepted it early in life, and I had created my reality accordingly.

In meditation, I discovered supporting beliefs that had contributed to my hypoglycemia. I used this information, along with what I had learned from my dream, to re-create my self as the healthy person I wanted to be. For the next year, I celebrated my self-healing nightly with rich, sugary treats (and gained 20 pounds—which I've since lost again).

INTERPRETING YOUR DREAMS

Many times the meaning of a dream is perfectly clear. For example, the significance of my "sweet" dream could hardly have been more obvious. Other times the meaning may not be immediately clear, but after careful examination, and with the use of some imagination, the significance is revealed.

Then there are those times when a dream seems to be nothing more than a chaotic, nonsensical fantasy. The principal reason for this is that we try to interpret dreams in the same manner that we interpret waking life. This doesn't always work. Unfettered by the laws of the physical world, dreams are a less restricted form of creative expression than waking experiences. In a dream we can grow from infancy to old age in seconds; we can travel from the earth to the moon by simply desiring to do so. A horse may instantly change into a sports car; a tenement in Harlem becomes a castle in Spain.

You can't hope to translate the words of a French-speaking waiter using an English/Chinese dictionary, and you can't expect to interpret a *seemingly* meaningless dream according to the symbols and organization of your physical life.

Some people try to solve this problem by buying a book that allegedly defines the meaning of dream symbols. These dream dictionaries, many of them relying heavily upon convoluted psychological generalizations, are basically useless. Each of us creates our own personal dream symbols. A banana in my dream may have an entirely different meaning than it does in a dream created by the author of one of these books. (I recently thumbed through two popular dream books. One of them claimed a banana held phallic significance; the other book said a banana meant the dreamer had a potassium deficiency.)

The main point I want to make about dream interpretation is that the best way to interpret your dreams is to learn the *personal* language and structure you use to create them. Start by identifying those dream symbols that correspond to the symbols that appear in your waking life. Compare the organization of your dream experiences, or the seeming lack of it, to the organization of waking events.

Examine a confusing dream during meditation or at another time when you're relaxed. Ask your self questions: "Did this dream provide me with an experience I've denied myself in waking life? Was the dream a mental creation of a fear, or a favorite fantasy? Was this a role-reversal dream? Did I change places with a friend, relative or co-worker to see what it's like to be in his shoes? What did I learn or express in this dream?

No dream is devoid of meaning, including those that initially appear to be absurd. With practice, you can become fluent in your personal dream language. Once you understand the meaning of your dream experiences you can use them to better create your life.

ADVENTURE 13

A DREAM ADVENTURE

STEP 1: Ask your self what you really believe about dreams, then list your beliefs. For example, do you believe dreams are therapeutic? Do you believe they are in any way important? Do you believe you can increase dream recall? Is it in your best interest to do so? Do you believe you can create specific dreams? From whom did you first accept your beliefs about dreams? What did that person really know about the dream state?

STEP 2: Temporarily turn your adventure logbook into a dream diary. For two weeks, use the method described in this chapter for increasing dream recall. Write down your remembered dreams each morning, then put a check mark next to those dreams that you believe to be somehow meaningful to your life.

STEP 3: After *faithfully* keeping your dream diary for two weeks, note the percentage of meaningful dreams.

STEP 4: List your current beliefs about dreams. Compare them with those beliefs you listed in Step 1, before logging your dreams. Do you *now* believe in the value of your dreams?

14

ACTING LIKE YOUR NEW SELF

In preceding chapters, we explored the powerful mental actions that can help you accept the new beliefs contained in your blueprint for personal change. This final chapter of Part Two is about using *physical* actions to help you become the person you want to be, living the life you desire.

Acting like your *new* self is an indispensable tool for change because mental action that isn't eventually followed by physical action is worthless when it comes to *Re-Creating Your Self*. Mentally affirming your *new* self is very helpful, but physically acting like your *new* self is essential.

When Shakespeare wrote, "Assume a virtue if you have it not," he could have been describing physical actions as a tool for personal change. When you physically affirm the person you want to become, you put wings on your positive mental actions. Acting like your *new* self demonstrates faith in your ability to become the kind of person you want to be, and you bring your self closer to becoming that person in fact.

If you have applied the principles of *Re-Creating Your Self* to your life, then you have already initiated important mental actions that will help you create the life you desire. However, on the physical level, you may still be acting in a manner that reinforces your old self.

For example, if your goal is to change a negative belief about your personal potential for prosperity, you can mentally affirm, "I am a magnet for money. I attract it effortlessly and in perfect ways." Indeed, your affirmation becomes a powerful tool for change. It immediately introduces a new point of view about your financial prospects. And every time you repeat the affirmation, your negative thoughts become less powerful and automatic. But ultimately, to really become "a magnet for money," your physical actions must corroborate your positive mental actions.

For instance, if you want to become prosperous but are poor right now, you may be mentally affirming prosperity but physically confirming poverty. Perhaps in your creative daydreams you act like Diamond Jim Brady, but in real life, you wouldn't think of reaching for a restaurant check— even a small one—because you still fear letting go of a buck.

Because you can't successfully re-create your self when your physical actions constantly contradict your positive mental actions, it's time to begin supporting your excellent mental efforts with similar physical actions. Now, don't get me wrong. In asking you to act like your *new* self, I'm not encouraging reckless or irresponsible behavior. If you're poor and want to become rich, I don't recommend going into hock to buy a pricey sports car in order to act like your prosperous *new* self.

A symbolic action is sufficient. If prosperity is your goal, then acting like your *new* self can be as easy as picking up the tab for coffee with a friend. Maybe it means donating one dollar to your favorite charity; perhaps you buy a 30-dollar garment you really like, instead of a less desirable 20-dollar sale item.

If your goal is self-trust, acting like your *new* self could mean making some small decision on your own that you would ordinarily not make without first consulting a friend. If self- love is the issue, you might do a little something each day to pamper your self: Have breakfast in bed, or take an extra few minutes to soak in a warm tub.

Your gesture need not be grand in order to be effective. Quite simply, your purpose is to deliberately take some action—no matter how small—that physically affirms your positive mental actions and demonstrates your willingness to change an old attitude.

A POWERFUL EXERCISE

You can begin acting like your *new* self right now, using a powerful technique that combines both mental and physical action to help you more quickly accept your new beliefs:

(1) Choose one of the new beliefs from your blueprint for personal change.
(2) Relax, then mentally affirm the belief for two or three minutes. (Use the affirmation you created for that particular belief in Adventure 10.)
(3) Immediately after affirming the belief, make it the theme of a creative daydream.

(4) After ending your creative daydream, take action to physically support your new belief. (Decide on the specific physical action before beginning this exercise. Remember, even a small gesture can be effective.)

This mental/physical exercise sends a powerful message to your self: It declares that—on all levels—you are ready, willing and able to accept a new kind of experience in your life.

TALKING LIKE YOUR *NEW* SELF

Talking like your *new* self is an important part of acting like your *new* self. Your words have great power. They can either help you become the person you want to be, or they can keep you in a rut. As Christ put it, "By thy words thou shalt be justified and by thy words thou shalt be condemned." He also taught that "death and life are in the power of the tongue."

Do the words you use in your conversations with others bring "death" to the negative beliefs you want to discard and give "life" to the person you want to become? If they don't, then they're undermining your efforts to re-create your self.

That was Allen's problem. In re-creating himself, Allen's primary goal was to change the negative beliefs that kept him from creating the relationship he desired.

Allen was lonely. He claimed that most women just weren't interested in him. The few women who showed interest didn't do so for long. Together we identified, examined and evaluated the beliefs that had created his negative experiences. On his own, Allen designed the blueprint for his *new* self; then he began using the tools for personal change.

So far, so good.

Three months after our final session, I received a phone call from a frustrated, angry Allen. In an accusing voice, he said that *Re-Creating Your Self* just wasn't working for him. His love life hadn't improved one iota. He continued to whine and complain, stopping short of asking for his money back. At first, Allen didn't take kindly to my suggestion that he return for one more session. But when I told him it would be "on the house," he grudgingly agreed.

Allen and I reviewed his blueprint for personal change. It was solid. He claimed that his self-love and self-trust continued to grow, if slowly. He was meditating daily. In creative daydreams, he saw himself in a happy, committed relationship with an attractive woman. Before going to sleep each night, he affirmed his *new* self. "I've done everything you suggested," he said. "So why haven't I created the relationship I want?"

"Are you *acting* like your *new* self?" I asked. "Do your words affirm the person you want to become?" Embarrassed, Allen admitted that although he was using all the other tools for change, he stopped short of physically supporting his new beliefs with appropriate words and action. In truth, his daily conversations reinforced the very beliefs he was trying to discard. For example, Allen would tell a friend about a girl he met at the gym. The friend would say, "Why didn't you ask her for a date?" Allen would answer, "Why would a beautiful girl like her want to go out with a guy like me?" Expressions such as "I don't stand a chance with her," "What do I have to offer a girl like that?" and "She's way out of my league" appeared with alarming frequency in his conversations.

Allen's words acted as powerful hypnotic suggestions that undermined his positive mental actions and reinforced his negative beliefs.

LISTEN TO YOUR SELF

If you want to know what you really believe at any given time, listen carefully to the words you use. They mirror your beliefs. They *are* your beliefs, orally expressed.

"If you can't say something good about someone, don't say anything at all." That's a cliche you would be wise to apply to your self: If you can't say something positive about your self, why say anything at all? There's no use in complaining, or belittling your self in conversation. It doesn't help you—it only strengthens your negative attitudes. And your wailing and whining are nothing but "ear pollution" to the person who's listening.

While understanding the importance of talking like their *new* selves, some students feel that to do so is to contradict their present reality. To them, this seems like lying. They're missing the point. I'm not suggesting that you lie. I'm asking you to choose your words more carefully. For instance, if you're broke and want to have money, don't reinforce your poverty-creating beliefs by saying, "I need a vacation...*but I can't afford it!*" Orally affirm the person you want to become by declaring, "I need a vacation, *and soon I'll be able to afford it!*"

Listen carefully to your self and the words you use regularly. At the same time, be careful not to spend too much time *listening* to people who make illness, failure or pessimism the principal themes of their conversations. Their negativity can be draining or, even worse, contagious.

Talking like your *new* self requires a conscious and deliberate effort on your part, at least for a while. That's because most of us have the bad habit of automatically dragging old words and negative phrases into our present conversations. With practice, talking like your *new* self will become as automatic and effortless as talking like your old self used to be.

ADVENTURE 14

ACTING LIKE MY <u>NEW</u> SELF

STEP 1: Open your logbook to Adventure 7, your blueprint for personal change, and review your new beliefs.

STEP 2: As you review, decide on one *simple* action you can take to physically affirm each belief. Under the heading, "Adventure 14 - Acting Like My *New* Self," list each new belief and the physical action you've chosen to support it. (Your guide provides a format you can use for this written step of the adventure.)

STEP 3: Each day put wings on one or more of your new beliefs by taking the physical action you decided on in Step 2. Continue until you have physically affirmed each belief at least once.

STEP 4: Think of a *new* way to physically support each of your new beliefs, then put your new ideas into action by repeating Step 3. Continue this process until acting like your *new* self becomes automatic.

YOUR GUIDE FOR ADVENTURE 14

AMY, 39 YEARS OLD:

When she first came to see me, Amy was a twice-divorced

137

businesswoman with a seventeen-year-old son and ten-year-old ulcers. "I already believe that I create my life," she said. "What I need to know now is how to create it in a way that will bring me some happiness and peace of mind."

RELATIONSHIPS
New belief: I trust Drew (Amy's boyfriend) *because, in the two years we've been dating, he's never given me a reason not to.*

Acting like my new self: *From now on, when talking to Drew on the phone, I will share the interesting things that have happened to me during the day. I will communicate my love and caring. In the past, I have spent most of our daily calls jealously giving Drew the third degree about his every action and personal encounter.*

MOTHERHOOD
New belief: *Being a good mother doesn't mean that I have to be my son's personal "slavey." In fact, I can become a better parent by making Michael assume responsibility.*

Acting like my new self: *I'm telling Michael that from now on he's responsible for cleaning his own room and washing his work uniforms.*

SELF-WORTH
New belief: *I am a good, valuable person right now. I don't need to prove my personal worth.*

Acting like my new self: *I'm going to stop belittling my employees when they make minor mistakes in order to increase my own sense of righteousness and personal worth.*

SELF-LOVE
New belief: *I love my self enough to sometimes allow pleasure to come before business.*

Acting like my new self: *Instead of paneling and reorganizing the garage next weekend, I'm going to accept Drew's offer of a romantic weekend in Catalina.*

PART THREE

A NEW LIFE,
A BETTER WORLD

15

YOUR LIFE CHANGES AS YOU RE-CREATE YOUR SELF

If you've read the first two parts of this book and completed the 14 "Adventures in Inner Space," then you know that the answers to your life are not in this, or any, book. They are not in any religious, scientific or political system, nor will they be found within any other person or thing.

The answers to your life are literally *within your self:* Your life springs from your inner experiences, and these are shaped by your personal beliefs. Those beliefs, along with the feelings, thoughts and expectations they generate, extend outward to create your life and all of its conditions. They alone determine your successes and failures, joys and sorrows, health and illnesses. If you're unhappy with any area of your life, you can change it by changing your beliefs.

The power to become the person you want to be, living the life you desire, is within you *now*. The *Re-Creating Your Self* process is a dynamic way of bringing that inner knowledge into your conscious awareness.

It is a goal of this process to return you to your rightful position of self-authority. You may have been conditioned to rely on the wisdom of others—parents, teachers, preachers, politicians and scientists—to define your personal reality and provide the framework for your life. Perhaps you've been encouraged to give authority over your self to some person, philosophy or "savior."

But the responsibility for your life is your own. Accept it. Only after you acknowledge that you are your own personal "savior" can you change the unsatisfying conditions of your life. You alone should decide upon the beliefs you are going to accept or reject, because the decisions you make will determine your life. If you want a fulfilling life, the beliefs you hold should add to your health, happiness and well-being. Regardless of the source, beliefs that create feelings of sinfulness, unworthiness, inadequacy, hate, fear, loss and lack should be rejected. These negative beliefs have never made anyone happy— and they never will!

Re-Creating Your Self reminds you that you are a good, highly creative individual—a person who has value and purpose. You are not, as some would have you believe, a sinful creature. Your life is not without worth and meaning.

You deserve the best life has to offer, and you have the power to create the best. Why accept anything less? There is nothing noble or spiritual about suffering and struggling. You are not here to "sweat and strain," to be punished for the sins of your ancestors or the transgressions of past lives. You are here to learn and grow, to enjoy and express your self, to create your experiences in a manner that is both personally enriching and inspirational to others. Acknowledging this alone can change your life. Maybe it already has.

EXPERIENCE IS YOUR BEST TEACHER

How does life work? What makes things happen? The scientific, religious and political systems that strongly influenced my childhood were unable to answer those essential questions to my satisfaction. These systems appeared to be handicapped by their own limited theories—theories that neither they nor I could prove. In other words, the prevailing scientific, religious and political systems of my youth asked me to accept their versions of "reality" on faith, not on firsthand experience. I found that unacceptable.

I believe that personal experience is the best teacher and the *only* acceptable criterion of truth. It must take precedence over all outside authority, conventional wisdom, secondhand testimony and cultural tradition. Many of you may feel the same way. That's why *Re-Creating Your Self* is structured in a manner that allows you to prove the validity of its principles for your self: first through the "Adventures in Inner Space," then through personal experience as you apply these ideas to your life.

When you ask, "How does life work, and what makes

things happen?", *Re-Creating Your Self* answers, "You create your life in line with your beliefs." From an infinite number of possibilities, you create your personal experiences according to your belief system. Seeing your beliefs manifested as physical events, you learn about your self. As your beliefs change, so do your experiences. You learn *new* things about your self; and by doing so, you grow and develop.

Understanding that you create your experiences, and knowing that you can alter them by altering your attitudes, can change your life even before you accept your new beliefs. However, to successfully re-create your self requires that you do more than acknowledge the value of these principles.

To become the person you want to be, living the life you desire, you must *use* these principles. You must apply this knowledge to your life. That is wisdom: *using* what you know to benefit your self and others.

Tragically, some people never use what they have learned to help themselves, much less others. They spend a lot of time, energy and money reading self-help books, attending lectures and seminars, going from one guru to another. They acquire knowledge, then put it on the shelf. You may have been one of these people in the past. You can change that right now.

The tools for personal change, explained in Part Two, will help toward that end. They can assist you in *using* what you have learned. If you use these tools regularly, your personal experiences will continue to improve; you will eventually achieve your goals. But if you use these tools erratically, on a hit-and-miss basis, you'll produce hit-and-miss results.

Students frequently ask, "Of all the tools for change, which are the most important?" Without hesitation, I answer, "Loving your self and thinking for your self." When you truly love your self, you know that you are innately good and eminently deserving of the best of everything. Then—and only then—do you create the best. When you think for your self, refusing to allow the limiting attitudes of others to determine the boundaries of your personal potential, then you are capable of fulfilling your heart's desires.

RE-CREATING YOUR *NEW* SELF

Your life changes as you re-create your self. As you come to accept your new beliefs, you are transformed from the other-created person you wrote about in Adventure 2 into the self-created individual you described in your blueprint for personal change. Your new, positive beliefs will create better experiences in all areas of your life and automatically attract other good beliefs.

Your re-created self is indeed new and improved—but don't expect to be perfect. Knowing the rules of a game, you can play it better, but this doesn't mean that you're going to achieve a perfect score. Similarly, knowing the rules of the game of life helps you to better create your life, but it doesn't mean you're going to become a perfect person.

In fact, "perfection" doesn't really exist in life; it's an illusion. "Perfection" implies *completion*—something that is finished and done. Check your dictionary: Perfection is a level of accomplishment beyond which there can be no further improvement and development. Thank goodness, no such "perfection" exists in this world.

Life involves you in the process of continually becoming more your self. For as long as you're alive, you're never finished. You are changed by every action. This process is endless, and you can make it endlessly exciting.

Even as you become the person you want to be, the *new* self you described in Adventure 7, you will naturally outgrow the goals you had set for your self; you will seek even higher levels of expression and achievement. Possibilities for further growth, development and creativity always exist, no matter how lofty your present accomplishments.

YOUR *BEST* SELF

Your challenge, then, is not to become "perfect" but to continually become *better*. Toward that end, you can use this book over and over again. Each reading will yield new and deeper insights into the life-determining principles of *Re-Creating Your Self*. Continued use of the tools for personal change will increase your ability to effectively make the changes you desire.

To become your *best* self, you must remain open to change. It's ironic. During childhood, we often embrace false and limiting beliefs from others before we have examined their value for ourselves. In adulthood, we frequently reject new attitudes that can improve our life before we have examined their value—*solely* because they don't agree with the limiting beliefs we've already accepted. Becoming your *best* self requires that you continually examine new ideas and old viewpoints, ask new questions, then go beyond the limits of your current beliefs to gain greater insights into your self, others and the world.

To become your *best* self, you must love the person you are right now, and at the same time, remember that no matter how much you've accomplished, it's only a beginning. Every moment brings another opportunity to re-create your self. Seize these opportunities. You shouldn't do less. You could hardly do more.

How will you be rewarded for your effort? Richly. Every day will bring you closer to becoming the person you want to be, living the life you desire. Health, happiness and prosperity can be yours to a degree you may have not believed possible. Though your life won't be without its challenges, you will better understand *how* and *why* you created your challenges, and how to triumph over them. On all levels, your life can become more creative, joyous and satisfying.

16

RE-CREATING THE WORLD

As I write this final chapter in July 1986, the world is still reeling from shock waves set off by a series of international catastrophes that began in January. Grim headlines are daily reminders that the world sorely needs re-creating if it is ever to become the kind of place where we can happily, healthfully and *safely* live the life we desire.

The past six months have seen some of the world's worst fears realized. We have experienced the frightening and tragic consequences of humankind's most negative beliefs made physically real.

In January, Americans watched in shocked disbelief as the space shuttle Challenger exploded 73 seconds after lift-off. In one nightmarish instant, six astronauts, a New Hampshire schoolteacher and the billion-dollar vehicle disappeared in a cloud of white smoke and orange fire.

That same month it was announced that AIDS had claimed its ten thousandth life. The epidemic was gaining a gruesome momentum, defying the experts and demonstrating that virtually *no one* was safe from this heinous virus.

Before winter ended there were other chilling reminders of our vulnerability. Airport terrorists in Rome and Vienna left eighteen dead and over 100 wounded. At home, supermarket terrorists laced our food and drugs with deadly cyanide.

Random violence and global tension blossomed in the spring. A terrorist bomb exploded aboard a jet over Greece, then a West Berlin disco was bombed, killing an American soldier. The next week, the United States retaliated by blasting military and intelligence targets in Tripoli. People feared that this strike would cause terrorism to escalate, or even worse, set off World War III.

Public anxiety and frustration peaked in May following an explosion and fire at a nuclear reactor in the Soviet Union. The Chernobyl disaster killed at least 31 people and injured countless others. It sent an invisible cloud of radioactivity around the world, contaminating people and animals, along with food and water supplies. Easily the worst catastrophe in the history of nuclear power, Chernobyl raised the prospect of long-term health and environmental damage. The International Atomic Energy Agency speculated that, over the next 70 years, up to 25,000 people in the western Soviet Union may die of cancers caused by the accident. Other authorities claimed that an additional 50,000 people *worldwide* may also develop fatal cancers due to the Chernobyl fallout.

World events during the first half of 1986 raised questions that are classic: Is science a savior or a saboteur? Is humankind defenseless against personal illness and global epidemics? Are aggression and violence innate ingredients in the nature of man, making war an inevitability? What will the future bring? Even more to the point, *will there be a future*?

During the writing of this book, these questions haunted my students and my friends. Some were overwhelmed by feelings of doom and despair. After Chernobyl, one dispirited student sent me a note, explaining why she wouldn't be returning for additional sessions: "Things seem to be going from bad to worse. What's the point of re-creating myself in a world that seems bent on destruction ... an *other*-created world that strongly believes in poverty, illness and war ... a world that doesn't value the individual or the planetary environment? The situation seems hopeless."

Later that same week, a teenage student approached the issue in a more positive way: "My parents grew up in the Sixties, and they thought they were going to change the world," he said. "Looking around, I sometimes feel pretty helpless to make the world a better place. It's so big, and such a mess. But I'm not ready to give up. Though I don't have my parents' innocent optimism, I still want to try to make a difference. Is there anything *I* can do to help re-create the world?"

My answer was a resounding, unqualified, "Yes!"

TOGETHER WE CREATE THE WORLD

You—the individual—can most definitely help re-create the world. In truth, you are even now contributing to the creation of the world you know.

Let me explain.

Individually, we create our personal experiences based on our beliefs.

Together, we create world events based upon our most powerful mass beliefs. The world outside is the cumulative result of the world within all individuals. It is a physical replica of humanity's combined inner beliefs and expectations—a mirror of what we are at any given time. Because the world outside reflects our inner development, as we are re-created, *it* is re-created.

You not only perceive and participate in your personal experiences, you create them. Likewise, you not only observe current events, you help shape them. Your personal beliefs, and the private and shared experiences they create, help form the world you know.

The beliefs of every individual, along with the feelings and expectations they produce, move out into society through mental and physical actions, coalescing to form world events. Everything that exists in the outer world first exists in the inner worlds of individuals.

Briefly, the process works like this: The beliefs of the individual create his personal experiences. The basic beliefs of all the individuals in a household come together to create their shared experiences. The prevailing beliefs of individual households merge to create what occurs in the neighborhood. The predominant beliefs of the collective neighborhoods determine what happens in a country. And the most powerful beliefs of individual countries combine to create world events.

But everything begins with the individual and his or her personal beliefs. It always has—and it always will. The private choices you make every day extend outward, affecting your household, your neighborhood, your country and your world. This is not meant to make you feel guilty or blameworthy for the woes of the world. It is meant to connect you with your power to help make things *better*.

The future of the world will not be decided by political, religious or scientific systems. It will not be determined by God, the stars or karma. For better or worse, the future of the world will be decided simply and solely by the personal choices that each of us make—and we will make those choices based upon our own personal beliefs. Therefore, if you want to take part in re-creating the world, the first and most meaningful step is to re-create your self.

CREATING A BETTER FUTURE

- We can create a better future when, individually and collectively, we understand that the future of the world begins on an individual level, then moves out into society. Our current beliefs have already formed today's world events and they are shaping tomorrow's.
- We can reform society when we fully recognize that society is composed of *individuals,* then acknowledge the basic integrity and value of *every* individual—even when outwardly that goodness is difficult to perceive.
- We can rid the world of evil only after we identify the true nature of "evil." Evil is not an inherent sinfulness or a natural tendency toward wickedness. Evil is ignorance—an ignorance that generates fear and pain, and causes humankind to violate the laws of nature, or, if you prefer, the laws of God. Ignorance, and not evil, is at the root of both personal and world problems.

SOME ANSWERS

Is science a savior or a saboteur? It is neither. Like everything else in this world, science, with its philosophy and technology, is but an outer manifestation of humankind's inner development.

Those who deify science, believing it will eventually end world hunger, eradicate illness and prevent wars, are in for a grave disappointment. Similarly, the religious shouldn't hold their collective breath waiting for a new savior, or the second coming of an old one, to step in and make the world right. It is the responsibility of the individual to create a better future—for himself, for others, and for the world. When we become dependent on *any* external source for our happiness—be it science, "savior," or a personal relationship, alcohol, drugs or material possessions—we shirk that basic self-responsibility.

We are sabotaged by science only to the extent that we sabotage ourselves. Because science mirrors our inner development, it can hardly be expected to demonstrate a loving regard for the well-being of people and the planet if, individually and collectively, we don't love ourselves and others. And for as long as we believe that aggression and violence are permissible, even necessary, to get what we want in our personal lives, science and society will reflect those mass beliefs by continuing to develop insidious weapons of destruction.

Is humankind the helpless victim of personal illness and mass epidemics? No. The AIDS virus, or any virus, may *carry* a disease—*but it doesn't cause the disease.* Whether you have a cold or a life-threatening illness, the disease doesn't come to you arbitrarily. Both personal illness and global epidemics are physical manifestations of inner dis-ease.

On the individual level, illness is often an outer manifestation of inner dis-ease over personal conditions that cause the quality of life to suffer. The physical symptoms may reflect inner frustration, unhappiness, or a feeling of hopelessness and despair. The malady may even be created as the result of false beliefs about disease itself, as was my former blood-sugar problem. On the world level, a mass epidemic is frequently the outer manifestation of widespread inner dis-ease caused by some economic, environmental, social or political situation. It may reflect the frustration, unhappiness or despair of an entire group of people.

Where the quality of life is good *on all levels*, no inner dis-ease exists, and neither do illnesses or epidemics. No individual or group of individuals become diseased unless the ailment serves some purpose.

When we come to realize that every sickness represents some form of inner dis-ease, then we can begin to eradicate illness in earnest. Instead of blaming outside circumstances and turning to science for the latest drug or vaccination to treat the *symptoms,* we will look within ourselves and eliminate the *source.*

WILL THERE BE A FUTURE?

Are violence and aggression inherent in the nature of man, making war an inevitability?

No.

Although we have long believed ourselves to be a naturally aggressive and violent species, and we have created world events based on that false belief, it is not a fact of life. It is a belief, and it can be changed. A Third World War is not an inevitability, nor is the nuclear destruction of the planet.

Interestingly, 1986, the same year that brought worldwide terrorism of unprecedented proportions, also brought an unexpected, but welcome, new attitude from the scientific community. The following statement was issued in Spain at the end of a Colloquium on Brain and Aggression sponsored by UNESCO. It represents the findings of scientists from 20 different fields of specialization:

"There is no scientific evidence to support the view

that, other things being equal, humans will behave aggressively ... It is scientifically incorrect to say that we have inherited from animals a tendency to make war; that war or violence is genetically programmed into human nature; that natural selection has favored aggressive behavior in human beings; that we have a 'violent brain' and that war is instinctive."

To their statement, I add that wars begin in the minds of men, and so does peace. Humankind has created wars according to some very powerful false beliefs, among them, a belief that aggression and violence are both instinctive and necessary ... a belief that the end justifies the means ... a belief that you can create good (peace) from bad (war) ... a belief that life is a competitive game, not a cooperative effort.

By changing these false beliefs, we can change the destructive and dehumanizing world events they create. The same species that created war is capable of creating peace. But world peace is dependent on individual peace. The answer to the question, "Will there be a future?" lies within each of us.

To change the world outside, you must first change the world within.

WHERE DO *YOU* BEGIN?

Start by identifying the social, political and economic conditions in the world that create the most powerful emotional reactions within you. Many times, you most strongly react to world problems that reflect your own personal challenges.

If you are passionate about environmental issues, look within your self to discover if "toxic" beliefs are polluting your inner environment. If they are, change your poisonous beliefs and you help change the world. If you would eradicate illness and epidemics, then begin by going within and healing any personal dis-ease.

Do you fervently desire an end to world poverty and hunger? You won't create abundance for others by denying your self what you need and want. Love and be generous with your self. Satisfy your own needs and desires, and you will automatically help others fulfill theirs.

If your goal is world peace, make the attainment of personal peace your first priority, then let it flow outward toward your neighbors, your country, and your world.

Virtually everything depends on you, the individual. If you are not re-created, then the world cannot be either, because the world is nothing more than the sum total of individuals in need of re-creation.

Can you change the world for the better?

Yes!

In fact, you already have. In a way that is both real and meaningful, you began re-creating the world when you started *Re-Creating Your Self.*

AFTERWORD

I enjoy hearing from people who have used *Re-Creating Your Self* to improve their lives. If you would like to write me about your personal experiences with this book, I encourage you to do so. I would be equally delighted to hear your suggestions for improving this process.

I am also available for lectures and private consultations. Write to:

CHRISTOPHER STONE
1313 BERYL ST., #A
REDONDO BEACH, CA 90277

❧ ❧ ❧

We hope you enjoyed this Hay House book.
If you would like to receive a free catalog featuring
additional Hay House books and products, or if you would
like information about the Hay Foundation, please contact:

Hay House, Inc.
P.O. Box 5100
Carlsbad, CA 92018-5100

(800) 654-5126
(800) 650-5115 (fax)

Please visit the Hay House Website at:
www.hayhouse.com

❧ ❧ ❧